ACTIVITY & TEST PREP WORKBOOK

SIDE by SIDE

THIRD EDITION

Steven J. Molinsky • Bill Bliss

with

Carolyn Graham

Contributing Authors

Dorothy Lynde • Elizabeth Handley

Illustrated by

Richard E. Hill

To the Teacher

This enhanced edition of *Side by Side Activity Workbook 3* provides all-skills activities, lifeskills lessons, and achievement tests to reinforce, expand, and assess the learning objectives in the *Side by Side 3* and *Side by Side Plus 3* Student Books. It includes two audio CDs and an answer key, providing students with the resources they need to extend their language learning through self-study outside the classroom. The audio CDs contain all workbook listening activities and GrammarRaps that motivate learners and promote language mastery through entertaining practice with rhythm, stress, and intonation.

The achievement tests in the second section of the workbook (pages T1–T54) provide intensified coverage of lifeskill competencies, assess student progress, and prepare students for the types of standardized tests and performance assessments used by many instructional programs. The tests include: multiple-choice questions that assess vocabulary, grammar, reading, listening skills, lifeskill competencies, and basic literacy tasks (such as reading classified ads, signs, and everyday documents); writing assessments that can be evaluated using a standardized scoring rubric and collected in portfolios of students' work; and speaking performance assessments designed to stimulate face-to-face interactions between students, for evaluation by the teacher using a standardized scoring rubric, or for self-evaluation by students. Test pages are perforated so that completed tests can be handed in and can serve as a record of students' participation and progress in the instructional program.

Listening scripts and answer keys for the tests are provided in *Side by Side Plus* Teacher's Guide 3. Test preparation strategies, scoring rubrics, and resources for documenting students' progress are provided in *Side by Side Plus* Multilevel Activity & Achievement Test Book 3 and its accompanying CD-ROM.

Side by Side, 3rd edition
Activity & Test Prep Workbook 3

Pearson Education, 10 Bank Street, White Plains, NY 10606
Editorial director: *Pam Fishman*
Vice president, director of design and production: *Rhea Banker*
Director of electronic production: *Aliza Greenblatt*
Production manager: *Ray Keating*
Director of manufacturing: *Patrice Fraccio*
Associate digital layout manager: *Paula Williams*

Associate art director: *Elizabeth Carlson*
Interior design: *Elizabeth Carlson, Wendy Wolf*
Cover design: *Elizabeth Carlson, Warren Fischbach*

The authors gratefully acknowledge the contribution of Tina Carver in the development of the original *Side by Side* program.

Printed in the United States of America
ISBN 978-0-13-040649-1; 0-13-040649-X

7 8 9 10 – V011 – 14 13

Contents

*Listening scripts and answer keys for the achievement tests are provided in *Side by Side Plus* Teacher's Guide 3.

A WHAT'S HAPPENING?

what	bake	cook	move	sit
where	compose	go	read	watch

1

1\. A. What's Fran reading?

B. She's reading her e-mail.

2\. A. Where's Fred ________?

B. ________ to the clinic.

3\. A. ________ Nancy ________?

B. ________ a game show.

4\. A. ________ you ________?

B. ________ dinner.

5\. A. ________ you and your wife ________?

B. ________ to Miami.

6\. A. ________ your grandmother and grandfather ________?

B. ________ in the park.

7\. A. ________ Victor ________?

B. ________ a symphony.

8\. A. ________ you ________?

B. ________ an apple pie.

B ON THE PHONE

1.

A. Hi. What ___are___ you doing?

B. ___I'm watching___ a movie on TV.

A. Oh. I don't want to disturb you. ______ Anna busy?

B. Yes, ____________. ________________ a bath.

A. I'll call back later.

2.

A. Hi, Bill. ________ the children okay?

B. Yes. __________ fine.

A. What ________________ doing?

B. Vicky ________________ her homework, and

Timmy ________________ baseball in the yard.

A. How about you? ____________________ doing?

B. __________________ dinner for you and the kids.

A. I'll be home soon.

3.

A. Hello, Peter. This is Mr. Taylor. ________ your father at home?

B. No, ____________. __________________ at the health club.

A. Can I speak to your mother?

B. I'm sorry. __________ busy right now. ______________ the washing machine. It's broken.

A. Okay. I'll call back later.

4.

A. Hello, ... Can I speak to ....?

B. I'm sorry. ....

A. Well, can I speak to ....?

B. I'm afraid ....

A. Okay. I'll call back later.

C YOU DECIDE: *Why Is Today Different?*

1. *(clean)* I never ___clean___ my apartment, but ___I'm cleaning___ it today because ___my grandmother is going to visit me *(or)* my boss is coming over for dinner___.

2. *(iron)* Roger never __________ his shirts, but __________ them today because __________.

3. *(argue)* We never __________ with our landlord, but __________ with him today because __________.

4. *(worry)* I never __________ about anything, but __________ today because __________.

5. *(watch)* Betty never __________ the news, but __________ it today because __________.

6. *(write)* Uncle Phil never __________ to us, but __________ to us today because __________.

7. *(take)* I never __________ the bus, but __________ it today because __________.

8. *(comb)* My son never __________ his hair, but __________ it today because __________.

9. *(get up)* My daughter never __________ early, but __________ early today because __________.

10. *(smile)* Mr. Grimes never __________, but __________ today because __________.

11. *(bark)* Our dogs never __________, but __________ today because __________.

12. *(wear)* Alice never __________ perfume, but __________ it today because __________.

D WHAT ARE THEY SAYING?

1.

2. My husband bakes delicious cakes. ________ he __________ pies, too?

3. My daughter gets up early. ________ your son __________ early, too?

4. They always complain about the traffic. ______ they __________ about the weather, too?

5. Maria speaks Italian and Spanish. ________ she __________ French, too?

6. My grandson lives in Miami. ______ your granddaughter ______ there, too?

7. I watch the news every morning. ________________________ every evening, too?

8. My sister plays soccer. ________________________ tennis, too?

9. Robert practices the trombone at night. ________________________ during the day, too?

10. We plant vegetables every year. ________________________ flowers, too?

11. Stanley always adds salt to the stew. ________________________ pepper, too?

12. I always wear a jacket to work. ________________________ a tie, too?

13. My cousin Sue rides a motorcycle. ________________________ a bicycle, too?

14. My grandfather jogs every day. ________________________ when it rains?

15. We need bread from the supermarket. ________________________ milk, too?

16. Gregory always irons his shirts. ________________________ his pants, too?

17.

E PUZZLE

Across

3. I like to cook. I'm an excellent ______.
4. I can type. I'm a very good ______.
5. Sally swims fast. She's a fast ______.
6. Jeff likes to play sports. He's a good ______.
7. My sons drive taxis. They're both taxi ______.

Down

1. You ski well. You're a very good ______.
2. We act in plays and movies. We're _____.
5. My children love to skate They're wonderful ______.

F WHAT'S THE ANSWER?

Circle the correct answer.

1. Does Hector like to play tennis?
   a. Yes, he likes.
   b. Yes, he does.
   c. Yes, he is.

2. Are you a graceful dancer?
   a. No, I don't.
   b. No, you aren't.
   c. No, I'm not.

3. Does your boss work hard?
   a. Yes, he is.
   b. Yes, he does.
   c. Yes, he works.

4. Is the food at this restaurant spicy?
   a. Yes, it isn't.
   b. Yes, it does.
   c. Yes, it is.

5. Are your children good athletes?
   a. Yes, I am.
   b. Yes, they are.
   c. Yes, they do.

6. Do you and your girlfriend like to cook?
   a. Yes, she does.
   b. Yes, they do.
   c. Yes, we do.

7. Am I a good teacher?
   a. Yes, you are.
   b. Yes, he is.
   c. Yes, you do.

8. Does your husband send e-mail messages to you?
   a. Yes, he is.
   b. Yes, he does.
   c. Yes, she does.

G WHAT ARE THEY SAYING?

1. A. I ___don't___ like to eat at Albert's house because he __________ cook very well.

   B. I know. Everybody says he ________ a very good ________.

2. A. I know you ________ like to drive with me because you think ________ a terrible driver.

   B. That's not true. I think you __________ very carefully!

3. A. __________ like to type?

   B. No, I ________. ________ not a very accurate typist.

   A. I disagree. __________ an accurate typist, but you ________ very slowly.

4. A. Oliver Jones is an excellent composer.

   B. I agree. He __________ beautifully. I think ________ very talented.

5. A. Irene ________ going swimming with us today because she __________ like to swim when it's cold.

   B. That's too bad. I really like to go swimming with her. She's a very good __________.

6. A. I'm jealous of my classmates. They speak English very well, and I ________.

   B. That's not true. Your classmates __________ English clearly, but you're a good English __________, too.

H LISTENING

Listen to each question and then complete the answer.

1. Yes, ___he does___.
2. No, ___she isn't___.
3. Yes, __________.
4. Yes, __________.
5. No, __________.
6. Yes, __________.
7. No, __________.
8. Yes, __________.
9. No, __________.
10. Yes, __________.
11. No, __________.
12. Yes, __________.
13. Yes, __________.
14. No, __________.
15. No, __________.

I GrammarRap: *Does He Like the Movies?*

Listen. Then clap and practice.

A. Does he like the movies?
B. No, he doesn't. He likes TV.

A. Does she like the mountains?
B. No, she doesn't. She likes the sea.

A. Do you like to hike?
B. No, I don't. I like to dive.

A. Do they like to walk?
B. No, they don't. They like to drive.

A. Is he studying music?
B. No, he isn't. He's studying math.

A. Is she taking a shower?
B. No, she isn't. She's taking a bath.

A. Are they living in Brooklyn?
B. No, they aren't. They're living in Queens.

A. Are you washing your shirt?
B. No, I'm not. I'm washing my jeans.

J WHAT'S THE QUESTION?

1. We're waiting for <u>the bus</u>.   *What are you waiting for?*
2. He's thinking about <u>his girlfriend</u>.   *Who is he thinking about?*
3. They're ironing <u>their shirts</u>. ______________________
4. I'm calling <u>my landlord</u>. ______________________
5. She's dancing with <u>her father</u>. ______________________
6. He's watching <u>the news</u>. ______________________
7. They're complaining about <u>the rent</u>. ______________________
8. She's playing baseball with <u>her son</u>. ______________________
9. They're visiting <u>their cousins</u>. ______________________
10. We're looking at <u>the animals in the zoo</u>. ______________________
11. I'm writing about <u>my favorite movie</u>. ______________________
12. He's arguing with <u>his boss</u>. ______________________
13. She's knitting a sweater for <u>her daughter</u>. ______________________
14. We're making <u>pancakes</u>. ______________________
15. I'm sending an e-mail to <u>my uncle</u>. ______________________
16. They're worrying about <u>their examination</u>. ______________________
17. She's talking to <u>the soccer coach</u>. ______________________
18. He's skating with <u>his grandparents</u>. ______________________

K WHAT ARE THEY SAYING?

1. A. Where are you and your husband taking your children?

   B. We're taking them to the zoo.

2. A. Why is Richard calling all __________ friends today?

   B. __________ wants to tell __________ about __________ new car.

3. A. What are your parents going to give you for your birthday?

   B. I'm not sure, but __________ might give __________ a puppy.

4. A. Why is Susie visiting __________ grandparents?

   B. __________ wants to show __________ her new bicycle.

5. A. Why are you wearing a safety helmet on __________ head?

   B. __________ don't want to hurt __________ head while I'm skateboarding.

6. A. Where are you taking __________ new girlfriend on Saturday night?

   B. __________ taking __________ to see the new science fiction movie downtown.

7. A. Why are those students complaining about their teacher?

   B. __________ think she gives __________ too much homework.

8. A. Can I tell you and Dad about the party now?

   B. No. We're sleeping now. You can tell __________ about __________ tomorrow morning.

9. A. Why is Mrs. Jenkins waiting for the plumber?

   B. The sink is leaking. Charlie, the plumber, says __________ can fix __________.

10. A. Timmy, why are you arguing with __________ sister?

    B. __________ wants to play with __________ new toys, but she can't. They're mine.

L WHAT'S THE WORD?

1. You should never argue [at / to / (with)] a police officer.
2. We're watching [at / to / (—)] a game show on TV.
3. You shouldn't shout [at / to / —] people.
4. Do you write [at / to / from] your keypals very often?
5. They always complain [at / — / about] the weather.
6. We visit [at / to / —] our sister's friends in Texas once a year.
7. I'm helping [at / to / —] my neighbors [to / with / —] their garden.
8. I'm always frustrated when I have to wait [for / — / at] the bus.
9. Call [to / — / at] the exterminator right away!

A HERBERT'S TERRIBLE DAY!

2

Herbert *(have)* __had__ [1] a very bad day yesterday. He usually gets up early, but yesterday morning he *(get up)* ________ [2] very late! He *(eat)* ________ [3] breakfast quickly, *(rush)* ________ [4] out of the house, and *(run)* ________ [5] to the bus stop. Unfortunately, he *(miss)* ________ [6] the bus. He *(wait)* ________ [7] for ten minutes, but there weren't any more buses, so he *(decide)* ________ [8] to walk to his office. Herbert was upset. He *(arrive)* ________ [9] at work two and a half hours late!

Herbert *(sit)* ________ [10] down at his desk and *(begin)* ________ [11] his work. He *(call)* ________ [12] a few people on the telephone, and he *(type)* ________ [13] a few letters. But he was in a hurry, and he *(make)* ________ [14] a lot of mistakes. He *(fix)* ________ [15] the mistakes, but when he *(finish)* ________ [16] the letters and *(put)* ________ [17] them on his desk, he *(spill)* ________ [18] water all over them.

At noon, Herbert *(go)* ________ [19] to the company cafeteria and *(order)* ________ [20] a pizza for lunch. That was a big mistake. The pizza was very spicy, and Herbert *(feel)* ________ [21] sick for the rest of the day.

Herbert's afternoon was even worse than his morning. He *(forget)* ________ [22] about an important meeting, his computer *(crash)* ________ [23], he *(fall)* ________ [24] asleep at his desk, his chair *(break)* ________ [25], and he *(hurt)* ________ [26] his arm.

Herbert *(leave)* ________ [27] the office at 5:00, *(take)* ________ [28] the bus home, and immediately *(go)* ________ [29] to bed! What a terrible, terrible day!

B LISTENING

Listen and circle the correct answer.

1.	yesterday / every day	4.	yesterday / every day	7.	yesterday / every day	10.	yesterday / every day
2.	yesterday / every day	5.	yesterday / every day	8.	yesterday / every day	11.	yesterday / every day
3.	yesterday / every day	6.	yesterday / every day	9.	yesterday / every day	12.	yesterday / every day

C WHAT'S THE WORD?

Fill in the missing words. Then read the story aloud.

decide	lift	need	paint	plant	roller-blade	wait	want

Last Saturday everyone wanted [1] my help. In the morning, I ____________ [2] heavy furniture for my wife, and I ____________ [3] the bathroom walls. Then I ____________ [4] in the park with my son and ____________ [5] flowers with my daughter. In the afternoon, my brother ____________ [6] my help. I went to a store with him and ____________ [7] while he ____________ [8] which suit to buy for his wedding.

D PUZZLE: *What Did They Do?*

Across

2. ride
3. teach
5. are
6. meet
7. deliver

Down

1. write
4. get
5. work

E WHAT'S THE QUESTION?

1.	Did you buy	the green one?	No, I didn't. I bought the blue one.
2.	______	a plane?	No, they didn't. They took a boat.
3.	______	a movie?	No, she didn't. She saw a play.
4.	______	French?	No, he didn't. He spoke Arabic.
5.	______	your arm?	No, I didn't. I broke my leg.
6.	______	at seven?	No, it didn't. It began at eight.
7.	______	to Paris?	No, she didn't. She flew to Rome.
8.	______	the beef?	No, we didn't. We had the chicken.
9.	______	with you?	No, they didn't. They went alone.
10.	______	too softly?	No, you didn't. You sang too loudly.
11.	______	your mother?	No, he didn't. He met my father.
12.	______	your keys?	No, I didn't. I lost my ring.

F WHAT'S THE ANSWER?

was	were
wasn't	weren't

angry	hungry	prepared	scared	tired
bored	on time	sad	thirsty	

1. The students fell asleep in Professor Winter's class because they were bored.
2. I didn't finish my sandwich today because I wasn't hungry.
3. They went to bed early last night because ______.
4. She didn't do well on the test because ______.
5. He shouted at them because ______.
6. I missed the train this morning because ______.
7. My daughter didn't finish all her milk because ______.
8. I covered my eyes during the movie because ______.
9. They cried when they said good-bye at the airport because ______.

G SOMETHING DIFFERENT

1. Albert usually drives very carefully.	He didn't drive carefully yesterday afternoon.	He drove much too fast.
2. Alice usually comes home from work early.	She __________ home early last night.	She __________ home late.
3. I usually take the bus to work.	I __________ the bus this morning.	I __________ the train.
4. We usually go to the movies on Saturday.	We __________ to the movies last Saturday.	We __________ to a concert.
5. Carl and Tom usually forget their homework.	They __________ their homework yesterday.	They __________ their lunch.
6. Mr. Tyler usually wears a suit to the office.	He __________ a suit today.	He __________ jeans.
7. Professor Hall usually teaches biology.	She __________ biology last semester.	She __________ astronomy.
8. Mr. and Mrs. Miller usually eat dinner at 7:00.	They __________ dinner at 7:00 last night.	They __________ at 9:00.
9. My grandmother usually gives me a tie for my birthday.	She __________ me a tie this year.	She __________ me a watch.
10. Alan usually sits by himself in English class.	He __________ by himself today.	He __________ with all his friends.
11. I usually have cereal for breakfast.	I __________ cereal this morning.	I __________ eggs.
12. Amanda usually sings very beautifully.	She __________ beautifully last night.	She __________ very badly.

H WHAT ARE THEY SAYING?

1. A. ___Did you___ clean your apartment this week?

   B. No, I ___didn't___. I ___was___ too lazy.

2. A. __________ meet the company president at the office party?

   B. No, we __________. But we __________ his wife.

3. A. __________ Richard fall?

   B. Yes, he __________. He skated very quickly, and he __________ very careful.

4. A. __________ Rita deliver all the pizzas today?

   B. No, __________. The people at 10 Main Street __________ home.

5. A. __________ Roger __________ asleep at the meeting this morning?

   B. No, __________. But he __________ asleep later in his office. He __________ very tired.

6. A. __________ you ride your motorcycle to work today?

   B. No, __________. I __________ my bicycle, and I __________ late. My supervisor __________ upset.

7. A. __________ like the movie?

B. Yes, I ________. It ________ great! How about you? Did you like it?

A. No, I __________. I thought it ________ boring.

8. A. ________ Mrs. Sanchez your Spanish teacher last semester?

B. Yes, she ________. ________ you in her class?

A. No, __________. I __________ take Spanish. I took French.

9. A. ________ you complain to your landlord about the problems in your apartment?

B. Yes, we ________. He listened to us, but he __________ fix anything. We __________ very angry.

10. A. ________ the students dance gracefully in the school play?

B. No, ____________. They __________ very awkwardly. They __________ very nervous.

11. A. Dad, ________ you buy anything at the supermarket?

B. Yes, __________. I __________ some food for dinner.

A. __________ buy any ice cream?

B. Sorry. I __________. There __________ any.

12. A. Grandpa, ________ you a good soccer player when you ________ young?

B. Yes, __________. I ________ a very good player. I ________ fast, and I __________ clumsy.

I HOW DID IT HAPPEN?

1. How did Steven sprain his ankle? *(play tennis)*

   He sprained his ankle while he was playing tennis.

2. How did your sister rip her pants? *(exercise)*

   ____

3. How did you break your arm? *(play volleyball)*

   ____

4. How did James poke himself in the eye? *(fix his sink)*

   ____

5. How did you and your brother hurt yourselves? *(skateboard)*

   ____

6. How did Mr. and Mrs. Davis trip and fall? *(dance)*

   ____

7. How did your father burn himself? *(cook french fries)*

   ____

8. How did your daughter get a black eye? *(fight with the kid across the street)*

   ____

9. How did you cut yourself? *(chop carrots)*

   ____

10. How did Robert lose his cell phone? *(jog in the park)*

    ____

11. How did you ______________________________?

    ____

J GrammarRap: *What Did He Do?*

Listen. Then clap and practice.

A. What did he do?
B. He did his homework.
A. What did she sing?
B. She sang a song.
A. What did they hide?
B. They hid their money.
A. Where did you go?
B. I went to Hong Kong.

A. What did he lose?
B. He lost his watch.
A. What did he study?
B. He studied French.
A. What did it cost?
B. It cost a lot.
A. What did they buy?
B. They bought a wrench.

K GrammarRap: *I Was Talking to Bob When I Ran Into Sue*

Listen. Then clap and practice.

I was talking to Bob when I ran into Sue.
I was waiting for Jack when I saw Mary Lou.
They were cleaning the house when I knocked on the door.
He was dusting a lamp when it fell on the floor.
She was learning to drive when I met her last May.
She was buying a car when I saw her today.

L WHAT'S THE QUESTION?

How	What	Where
How long	What kind of	Who
How many	When	Why

1.	Who did you meet?	I met the president.
2.		She lost her purse.
3.		We did our exercises at the beach.
4.		They left at 9:15.
5.		She got here by plane.
6.		He sang in a concert hall.
7.		They stayed for a week.
8.		I saw a science fiction movie.
9.		He cried because the movie was sad.
10.		She wrote a letter to her brother.
11.		They complained about the telephone bill.
12.		We ate a lot of grapes.
13.		He spoke at the meeting.
14.		They lifted weights all morning.
15.		She gave a present to her cousin.
16.		I ordered apple pie.
17.		We rented seven videos.
18.		They sent an e-mail to their teacher.
19.		He fell asleep during the lecture.
20.		I lost my hat while I was skiing.

M OUR VACATION

1. A. Did you go to Hong Kong?

   B. No, ___we didn't___.

   A. Where ___did you go___?

   B. ___We went___ to Tokyo.

2. A. Did you get there by boat?

   B. No, ______________.

   A. How ______________________?

   B. ______________________.

3. A. Did your flight to Japan leave on time?

   B. No, ______________.

   A. How late ______________________

   ______________________?

   B. ______________ two hours late.

4. A. Did you have good weather during the flight?

   B. No, ______________.

   A. What kind of ______________________

   ______________________?

   B. ______________ terrible weather.

5. A. Did you stay in a big hotel?

   B. No, ______________.

   A. What kind of ______________________

   ______________________?

   B. ______________________.

6. A. Did you eat American food?

   B. No, ______________.

   A. What kind of ______________________

   ______________________?

   B. ______________________.

(continued)

7. A. Did you take your camera with you?

B. No, ________________.

A. What ______________________________

________________________________?

B. ____________ our camcorder.

8. A. Did you get around the city by train?

B. No, ________________.

A. How ______________________________

________________________________?

B. ________________________________.

9. A. Did you meet many Japanese?

B. No, ________________.

A. Who ______________________________?

B. __________________ other tourists.

10. A. Did you buy any clothing?

B. No, ________________.

A. What ______________________________?

B. ______________________ souvenirs.

11. A. Did you speak Japanese?

B. No, ________________.

A. What language __________________

________________________________?

B. ________________________________.

12. A. Did you spend a lot of money?

B. Yes, ________________.

A. How much ______________________

________________________________?

B. ________________________________.

N SOUND IT OUT!

Listen to each word and then say it.

this				these		
1. chicken	3. river	5. busy		1. cheese	3. asleep	5. Steve
2. middle	4. kid	6. didn't		2. meat	4. receive	6. repeat

Listen and put a circle around the word that has the same sound.

1. clean: fine middle these
2. mix: ski did need
3. easy: Rita break eyes
4. video: machine big keep
5. east: build little green
6. symphony: mittens life retire
7. rip: knee maybe knit

Now make a sentence using all the words you circled, and read the sentence aloud.

8. ______ ______ ______ ______ ______ ______ ______

9. meat: Greek Internet eight
10. spill: healthy his rainy
11. promise: child key Richard
12. tea: every men into
13. cookie: with speaks bricks
14. milk: mine advice with
15. team: is week attractive
16. typical: sister lazy rebuild

Now make a sentence using all the words you circled, and read the sentence aloud.

17. ______ ______ ______ ______ ______ ______ ______ ______

3

A WHAT ARE THEY SAYING?

1. A. Did you ride your bicycle to work this morning?

   B. No, I didn't. I rode my motorcycle. I'm going to ride my bicycle to work tomorrow morning.

2. A. Did Tommy wear his new shoes to school today?

   B. ______________. He ________ his old shoes. ______________ his new shoes tomorrow.

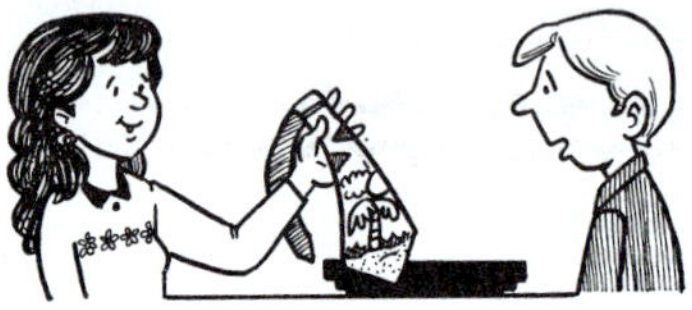

3. A. Did Sally give her husband a sweater for his birthday this year?

   B. ______________. She ________ him a tie. ______________ him a sweater next year.

4. A. Did your parents drive to the mountains last weekend?

   B. ______________. They ________ to the beach. ______________ to the mountains next weekend.

5. A. Did you and your family have eggs for breakfast this morning?

   B. ______________. We ________ pancakes. ______________ eggs tomorrow morning.

6. A. Did you go out with Mandy last Saturday night?

   B. ______________. I ________ out with Sandy. ______________ out with Mandy next Saturday night.

7. A. Did Howard write an interesting story for homework today?

   B. ______________. He ________ a boring one. ______________ a more interesting story next time.

8. A. Did Shirley leave the office early this afternoon?

   B. ______________. She ________ very late. ______________ early tomorrow afternoon.

B BAD CONNECTIONS!

1.

I'm really scared. Tomorrow my dentist is going to ###########.

I'm sorry. I can't hear you. I think we have a bad connection. What's ___your dentist going to do___?

2.

We're very excited about our trip. We're going to go to ############.

What did you say? I can't hear you. Where ______________ ______________________?

3.

My son is very sad. His girlfriend is going to move to Alaska because #############.

I'm sorry. We have a bad connection. Why __________ ______________________?

4.

My parents are going to give me a ############ for my sixteenth birthday.

Excuse me. I can't hear you. ______________________ ______________________?

5.

I'm really nervous. I'm going to ############ for the first time tomorrow.

We have a bad connection. ______________________ ______________________?

6.

Please come to our wedding. We're going to get married next ############.

I'm sorry. I can't hear you. ______________________ ______________________?

7.

I won't be home after school today. I'm going to meet ############.

This is a terrible connection! ______________________ ______________________?

(continued)

8.

9.

10.

11.

12.

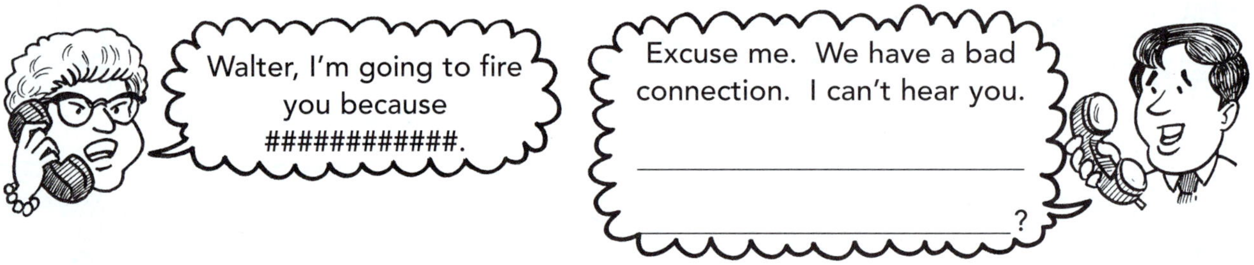

C LISTENING

Listen and choose the time of the action.

1. a. last night
   (b.) tomorrow night
2. a. yesterday afternoon
   b. tomorrow afternoon
3. a. this weekend
   b. last weekend
4. a. this Saturday
   b. last Saturday
5. a. last week
   b. next week
6. a. yesterday evening
   b. this evening
7. a. tomorrow night
   b. last night
8. a. this weekend
   b. last weekend
9. a. this evening
   b. yesterday evening
10. a. last winter
    b. this winter
11. a. tomorrow morning
    b. yesterday morning
12. a. next semester
    b. last semester

D THE PESSIMIST AND THE OPTIMISTS

James is a pessimist. He always thinks the worst will happen.

All his friends are optimists. They always tell James he shouldn't worry.

1. I'm afraid I ___won't have___ a good time at the office party tomorrow.
   Yes, ___you will___. ___You'll___ have a wonderful time.

2. I'm sure my son ___will hurt___ himself in his soccer match today.
   No, ___he won't___. ___He won't___ hurt himself. He's always very careful.

3. I'm afraid my grandmother ______________ get out of the hospital soon.
   Yes, ______________. ______________ get out of the hospital in a few days.

4. I'm afraid my wife ______________ upset if I get a very short haircut.
   No, ______________. ______________ be upset.

5. I'm positive I ______________ weight on my new diet.
   Yes, ______________. ______________ lose a lot of weight.

6. I'm afraid my children ______________ my birthday this year.
   No, ______________. ______________ forget your birthday. They never forget it.

7. I'm afraid my landlord ______________ our broken doorbell.
   Yes, ______________. ______________ fix it as soon as he can.

8. I'm afraid my new neighbors ______________ like me.
   Of course ______________. ______________ you a lot. Everybody likes you.

9. I'm sure ________ catch a cold when we go camping this weekend.
   No, ______________. ______________ catch a cold, James. You worry too much!

E WHAT WILL BE HAPPENING?

attend   browse   clean   do   fill out   rain   watch   work out

1. A. Will Amanda be busy this afternoon?

   B. Yes, ___she will___.

   ___She'll be doing___ research at the library.

2. A. Will you be busy this evening?

   B. Yes, __________. __________

   __________ my income tax form.

3. A. Will Donald be home this afternoon?

   B. No, __________. __________

   __________ at his health club.

4. A. Will Mr. and Mrs. Lee be busy tonight?

   B. Yes, __________. __________

   __________ their apartment.

5. A. Will Grandpa be busy tonight?

   B. Yes, __________. __________

   __________ the web until after midnight.

6. A. Will you and your wife be home today?

   B. Yes, __________. __________

   __________ our favorite game show on TV.

7. A. Will Mom be home early tonight?

   B. No, __________. __________

   __________ a meeting.

8. A. Will the weather be nice this weekend?

   B. No, __________. __________

   __________ cats and dogs!

F A TOUR OF MY CITY

Pretend you're taking people on a tour of your city or town. Fill in the blanks with real places you know.

Good morning, everybody. This is ______________ speaking. I'm so glad you'll be coming with me today on a tour of ______________. We'll be leaving in just a few minutes.

First, I'll be taking you to see my favorite places in the city: ______________, ______________, and ______________. Then we'll be going to ______________ for lunch. In my opinion, this is the best restaurant in town. After that, I'll be taking you to see the other interesting tourist sights: ______________, ______________, and ______________. This evening we'll be going to ______________. I'm sure you'll have a wonderful time.

G WHAT ARE THEY SAYING?

1. A. I'm sorry. I can't talk right now. I'm ___giving___ the kids a bath.

   B. How much longer ___will you be giving___ them a bath?

2. A. How much longer ______________ ______________ your homework?

   B. I'll probably ______________ my homework for another half hour.

   A. Okay. I'll call you then.

3. A. Hi, Carol. This is Bob. Can you ______________ for a minute?

   B. Sorry. I can't ______________ right now. I'm ______________ for a big test.

4. A. Sorry, Alan. I can't talk now. I'm ______________ dinner with my family.

   B. How much longer ______________ ______________ dinner?

H GrammarRap: *Will They Be Home?* 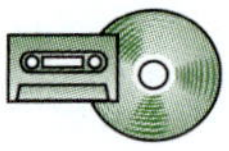

Listen. Then clap and practice.

A.	Will you	be home	at a quarter	to three?
B.	Yes,	I will.	I'll be watching	TV.

A.	Will John	be home	at half	past two?
B.	Yes,	he will.	He'll be cooking	some stew.

A.	Will your parents	be home	today	at four?
B.	Yes,	they will.	They'll be washing	the floor.

A.	Will Jane	be home	if I call	at one?
B.	Yes,	she will.	She'll be feeding	her son.

A.	Will you	be home	at half	past eight?
B.	No,	I won't.	I'll be working	late.

A.	Will John	be home	at a quarter	to ten?
B.	No,	he won't.	He'll be visiting	a friend.

A.	Will your parents	be home	tonight	at nine?
B.	No,	they won't.	They'll be standing	in line.

A.	Will Jane	be home	if I call her	at seven?
B.	No,	she won't.	She'll be dancing	with Kevin.

I WHOSE IS IT?

mine	his	hers	ours	yours	theirs

A. Hi, Robert. I found this wallet in my office today. Is it ___yours___ 1?

B. No, it isn't ____________ 2, but it might be Tom's.

A. Maybe, but Tom hardly ever visits my office. It probably isn't ____________ 3.

B. It's small and blue. Maybe it's Martha's.

A. I asked her this morning. She says it isn't ____________ 4.

B. Is there anything inside the wallet?

A. There isn't any money, but there's a picture of three children.

B. It might belong to Mr. Hill. He and his wife have three children. Maybe the children are ____________ 5.

A. I showed the picture to Mr. and Mrs. Hill. They said, "These children aren't ____________ 6. Our children are older."

B. Maybe you should give the wallet to our supervisor.

A. You know, it might be ____________ 7. She has three children!

B. You're right. I'm positive it's ____________ 8. I saw her children in her office last week.

J GRAMMARRAP: *Where's My Coat?*

Listen. Then clap and practice.

A. Where's my coat? I can't find mine.
Is this one mine or yours?
B. That one is mine. It isn't yours.
Yours is next to those doors.

A. Where's our umbrella? We can't find ours.
Is this one ours or theirs?
B. That one is theirs. It isn't yours.
Yours is under those chairs.

K WHAT DOES IT MEAN?

Circle the correct answer.

1. Jim is wearing a tuxedo today.
   a. He's going to visit his grandmother.
   (b.) He's going to a wedding.
   c. He's going to work in a factory.

2. My brother has a black eye.
   a. He painted his eye.
   b. He's wearing dark glasses.
   c. He hurt his eye.

3. The teacher wasn't on time.
   a. She was early.
   b. She was late.
   c. She didn't have a good time.

4. They chatted online yesterday.
   a. They used a cell phone.
   b. They used a computer.
   c. They used a fax machine.

5. Everyone in my family is going to relax this weekend.
   a. We're going to rest this weekend.
   b. We're going to retire this weekend.
   c. We're going to return this weekend.

6. He wasn't prepared for his exam.
   a. He didn't study for the exam.
   b. He didn't take the exam.
   c. He was ready for the exam.

7. Could I ask you a favor?
   a. I want to help you.
   b. I want to give you something.
   c. I need your help.

8. It's a very emotional day for Janet.
   a. She's going to work.
   b. She's getting married.
   c. She's studying.

9. He's composing a symphony.
   a. He's writing a symphony.
   b. He's listening to a symphony.
   c. He's going to a concert.

10. George ripped his shirt.
    a. He has to wash his shirt.
    b. He has to iron his shirt.
    c. He has to sew his shirt.

11. Can I borrow your bicycle?
    a. I need your bicycle for a little while.
    b. I want to give you my bicycle.
    c. I want to buy your bicycle.

12. Every day I practice ballet.
    a. I sing every day.
    b. I play violin every day.
    c. I dance every day.

13. I'm going to lend my car to Bob today.
    a. Bob is going to drive my car.
    b. I'm going to drive Bob's car.
    c. Bob is going to give me his car.

14. Mr. and Mrs. Hansen love to talk about their grandchildren.
    a. They listen to them.
    b. They're very proud of them.
    c. They argue with them.

15. Rita did very well on her exam.
    a. She's happy.
    b. She's anxious.
    c. She's sad.

16. I'm going to repair my washing machine.
    a. I'm going to paint it.
    b. I'm going to fix it.
    c. I'm going to do laundry.

17. I need to assemble my new VCR.
    a. Can I borrow your screwdriver?
    b. Can I borrow your ladder?
    c. Can I borrow your TV?

18. I sprained my ankle.
    a. I broke my ankle.
    b. I hurt my ankle.
    c. I poked my ankle.

19. I'm going to fill out my income tax form.
  a. I'm going to return it.
  b. I'm going to read it.
  c. I'm going to answer the questions on the form.

20. They're playing Scrabble.
  a. They're playing a game.
  b. They're playing a sport.
  c. They're playing an instrument.

21. Mr. Smith is complaining to his boss.
  a. He's talking about his boss, and he's upset.
  b. He's talking to his boss, and he's happy.
  c. He's talking to his boss, and he's upset.

22. I'm going to call my wife right away.
  a. I'm going to call her immediately.
  b. I'm going to call her in a few hours.
  c. I'm going to call her when I have time.

23. My sister is an excellent athlete.
  a. She's an active person.
  b. She plays sports very well.
  c. She likes to watch sports.

24. My mother is looking forward to her retirement.
  a. She's happy about her new job.
  b. She wants to buy new tires for her car.
  c. Soon she won't have to go to work every day.

L LISTENING: *Looking Forward*

Listen to each story. Then answer the questions.

What Are Mr. and Mrs. Miller Looking Forward to?

1. Mr. and Mrs. Miller _____ last week.
  (a.) moved
  b. relaxed
  c. flew to Los Angeles

2. Mr. and Mrs. Miller aren't going to _____ this weekend.
  a. repaint their living room
  b. assemble their VCR
  c. relax in their yard

3. They're going to _____ next weekend.
  a. assemble their computer
  b. relax
  c. paint flowers

What's Jonathan Looking Forward to?

4. Jonathan isn't _____ today.
  a. sitting in his office
  b. thinking about his work
  c. thinking about next weekend

5. Next weekend he'll be _____.
  a. working
  b. cooking and cleaning
  c. getting married

6. On their trip to Hawaii, Jonathan and his wife won't be _____.
  a. swimming in the ocean
  b. paying bills
  c. eating in restaurants

What's Mrs. Grant Looking Forward to?

7. When she retires, Mrs. Grant will be _____.
  a. getting up early
  b. getting up late
  c. taking the bus to work

8. Mrs. Grant will _____ with her friends.
  a. go to museums
  b. work in her garden
  c. read books

9. She'll take her grandchildren to _____.
  a. the park and the beach
  b. the zoo and the beach
  c. the park and the zoo

✓ CHECK-UP TEST: Chapters 1–3

A. Fill in the blanks.

Ex. Ann ___is___ a good skater, and her children ___skate___ well, too.

1. A. Mr. and Mrs. Lee ________ wonderful dancers.
   B. I agree with you. They ____________ very well.
2. A. Roger ____________ very carelessly.
   B. I know. He's a terrible driver.
3. A. We don't swim very well.
   B. I disagree. I think ________ excellent ______________.
4. A. I type very well. I think ________ a very good ____________.
5. A. We ________ good ____________, but we like to ski anyway.

B. Fill in the blanks.

1. A. Did you speak to Mrs. Baxter yesterday?
   B. No, I __________. I ________ too busy. But I __________ to Mrs. Parker.
2. A. Did you buy juice when you were at the store?
   B. No, I __________. I forgot. But I __________ milk.
3. A. __________ they get up early this morning?
   B. No, they __________. They ______ up very late.
4. A. Did Mr. Wong teach biology last semester?
   B. No, he __________. He __________ astronomy because the astronomy teacher ________ sick all semester.
5. A. __________ you talk to Tom last night?
   B. No, I __________. I __________ to his wife. Tom __________ there when I called.

C. Write the questions.

Ex. We're arguing with our landlord.
___Who are you arguing with?___

1. I'm writing about my favorite movie.
   ____
2. They're going to fix their bookcase.
   ____
3. He hiked in the mountains.
   ____
4. She'll be ready in a few minutes.
   ____
5. They arrived by plane.
   ____
6. We'll be staying until Monday.
   ____
7. She's going to hire five people.
   ____

D. Answer the questions.

Ex. What did your daughter do yesterday morning?

(do her homework) She did her homework.

1. What's your sister doing today?

   (adjust her satellite dish) ______

2. What does your brother do every evening?

   (chat online) ______

3. What are you going to do next weekend?

   (visit my mother-in-law) ______

4. What did Jack and Rick do yesterday afternoon?

   (deliver groceries) ______

5. What was David doing when his children came home from school?

   (bake a cake) ______

6. How will you get to work tomorrow?

   (take the bus) ______

7. What will you and your husband be doing this evening?

   (watch TV) ______

8. How did you cut your hand?

   (chop carrots) ______

E. Listen to each question and then complete the answer.

Ex. Yes, he does.

1. Yes, ______.
2. No, ______.
3. Yes, ______.
4. Yes, ______.
5. No, ______.
6. Yes, ______.
7. No, ______.
8. Yes, ______.

4

A FOR MANY YEARS

1. I ride horses.

   I've ridden horses for many years.

2. I fly airplanes.

   __________ airplanes for several years.

3. I give injections at the hospital.

   __________ injections for many years.

4. I speak Italian.

   __________ it all my life.

5. I take photographs.

   __________ them for many years.

6. I do exercises every day.

   __________ them every day for many years.

7. I draw cartoons.

   __________ cartoons for several years.

8. I write for a newspaper.

   __________ for a newspaper for many years.

9. I drive carefully.

   __________ carefully all my life.

B LISTENING

Listen and choose the word you hear.

1. (a.) ridden b. written
2. a. taking b. taken
3. a. giving b. given
4. a. written b. driven
5. a. writing b. written
6. a. drawing b. doing
7. a. spoken b. speaking
8. a. done b. drawn

C I'VE NEVER

be	fly	give	ride	sing	take
draw	get	go	see	swim	write

1. I've never flown in a helicopter.

2. ______________ a raise.

3. ______________ in a limousine.

4. ______________ a cartoon.

5. ______________ a book.

6. ______________ a trip to Hawaii.

7. ______________ in a choir.

8. ______________ in the Mediterranean.

9. ______________ on television.

10. ______________ on a cruise.

11. ______________ a present to my teacher.

12. ______________ a Broadway show.

D LISTENING

Is Speaker B answering *Yes* or *No*? Listen to each conversation and circle the correct answer.

1.	(Yes) No	3.	Yes No	5.	Yes No	7.	Yes No
2.	Yes No	4.	Yes No	6.	Yes No	8.	Yes No

E WHAT ARE THEY SAYING?

fall	get	give	go	ride	wear

1. A. ___Have you ever gotten___ stuck in bad traffic?
   B. Yes. As a matter of fact, ___I got___ stuck in very bad traffic this morning.
2. A. ______________________ on a Ferris wheel?
   B. Yes, I have. __________ on a Ferris wheel last weekend.
3. A. ______________________ a tuxedo?
   B. Yes, I have. __________ a tuxedo to my sister's wedding.
4. A. ______________________ scuba diving?
   B. Yes, I have. __________ scuba diving last summer.
5. A. ______________________ blood?
   B. Yes, I have. __________ blood a few months ago.
6. A. ______________________ on the sidewalk?
   B. Yes. In fact, __________ on the sidewalk a few days ago.

F GRAMMARRAP: *Have You Ever?*

Listen. Then clap and practice.

A. Have you ever • seen • a rainbow? • •
Have you ever • learned • to dance? • •
Have you ever • flown • an airplane? • •
Have you ever • gone • to France? • •

B. No, I've never • seen • a rainbow. • •
I've never • learned • to dance. • •
I've never • flown • an airplane. • •
But I've often • gone • to France. • •

G WHAT ARE THEY SAYING?

drive	eat	go	meet	see	speak	take	write

1. A. Have your children eaten breakfast yet?

   B. Yes, they have. They ate breakfast a little while ago.

2. A. ________ George ________ his new car yet?

   B. Yes, ________. ________ it for the first time this morning.

3. A. ________ Gloria ________ to the post office yet?

   B. Yes, ________. ________ to the post office a little while ago.

4. A. ________ you and Jane ________ the new movie at the Westville Mall?

   B. Yes, ________. ________ it last Saturday night.

5. A. ________ the employees ________ inventory yet?

   B. Yes, ________. ________ inventory last weekend.

6. A. ________ you ________ to the landlord yet?

   B. Yes, ________. ________ to him this morning.

7. A. ________ I ________ a letter to the Carter Company yet?

   B. Yes, ________. ________ them a letter last week.

8. A. ________ you and your wife ________ your daughter's new boyfriend yet?

   B. Yes, ________. ________ him last Friday night.

H NOT TODAY

1. Kenji and his girlfriend aren't going to eat at Burger Town today. __They've__ already __eaten__ at Burger Town this week. __They ate__ there on Monday.

2. My sister isn't going dancing tonight. ________ already ________ dancing this week. ____________ dancing last night.

3. Timothy isn't going to wear his new jacket to work today. ________ already ________ it to work this week. ____________ it yesterday.

4. My husband and I aren't going to do our laundry today. ________ already ________ our laundry this week. ____________ it on Saturday.

5. Roger isn't going to give his girlfriend candy today. ________ already ________ her candy this week. ____________ her candy yesterday morning.

6. I'm not going to see a movie today. ________ already ________ a movie this week. ____________ a movie on Wednesday.

7. We aren't going to buy fruit at the supermarket today. ________ already ________ fruit at the supermarket this week. ____________ some fruit two days ago.

8. Susie isn't going to visit her grandparents today. ________ already ________ them this week. ____________ them yesterday.

9. David isn't going to take his children to the circus today. ________ already ________ them to the circus this week. ____________ them to the circus a few days ago.

I WHAT'S THE WORD?

go went gone

1. We should ___go___ now.
2. They ___went___ home early today.
3. She's already ___gone___ home.

see saw seen

4. I've never __________ him.
5. I __________ her yesterday.
6. Do you __________ them often?

eat ate eaten

7. I __________ there this morning.
8. Has he ever __________ there?
9. Do you __________ there every day?

write wrote written

10. How often do you __________ to them?
11. She's already __________ her report.
12. He __________ her a very long letter.

wear wore worn

13. When will you __________ it?
14. He's never __________ it.
15. She __________ it today.

speak spoke spoken

16. Who __________ to you about it?
17. She can't __________ Chinese.
18. Have they __________ to you?

drive drove driven

19. They've never __________ there.
20. We never like to __________ there.
21. She __________ there today.

do did done

22. Did you __________ your homework?
23. We __________ that yesterday.
24. Have you ever __________ that?

J WHAT ARE THEY SAYING?

1. A. Janet, you've got to do your homework.

   B. But, Mother, <u>I've</u> already __________ my homework today.

   A. Really? When?

   B. Don't you remember? ____________ my homework this afternoon.

   A. Oh, that's right. Also, __________ you ______________ a letter to Grandma yet?

   B. Yes, __________. I wrote to her yesterday.

2. A. Would you like to swim at the health club tonight?

   B. I don't think so. _______ already ___________ at the health club today.

   A. Really? When?

   B. ______________ there this morning.

3. A. Are you going to take your vitamins?

   B. ________ already ____________ them.

   A. Really? When?

   B. ______________ them before breakfast.

   How about you? ________ you ____________ yours?

   A. Yes, __________. I __________ mine when I got up.

4. A. I hope Jimmy gets a haircut soon.

   B. Don't worry, Mother. ______ already _________ one.

   A. I'm glad to hear that. When?

   B. ______________ a haircut yesterday.

   A. That's wonderful!

5. A. When are you and Fred going to eat at the new restaurant downtown?

B. __________ already ____________ there.

A. Really? When?

B. ______________ there last weekend.

A. How was the food?

B. It was terrible. It was the worst food we've ever __________!

6. A. When are you going to speak to the boss about a raise?

B. ________ already ______________ to her.

A. Really? When?

B. ______________ to her this morning.

A. What did she say?

B. She said, "..."

K GRAMMARRAP: *Have You Gone to the Bank?*

Listen. Then clap and practice.

A. Have you gone to the bank?

B. Yes, I have.

I went to the bank at noon.

A. Have they taken a vacation?

B. Yes, they have.

They took a vacation in June.

A. Has he written the letters?

B. Yes, he has.

He wrote the letters today.

A. Has she gotten a raise?

B. Yes, she has.

She got a raise last May.

L IN A LONG TIME

buy	dance	fly	go	read	see	swim
clean	eat	give	make	ride	study	take

1. A. What's the matter, Susan? You aren't riding very well today.

   B. I know. I haven't ridden in a long time.

2. A. I can't believe it! These cars are very expensive.

   B. Remember, we ______________ a new car in a long time.

3. A. Are you nervous?

   B. Yes, I am. ______________ in an airplane in a long time.

4. A. Are you excited about your vacation?

   B. Yes, I am. ______________ a vacation in a long time.

5. A. You aren't swimming very well today.

   B. I know. ______________ in a long time.

6. A. Buster is really hungry.

   B. I know. He ______________ anything in a long time.

7. A. Susie's room is very dirty.

   B. I know. She ______________ it in a long time.

8. A. I think Timmy watches too much TV.

   B. You're right. ______________ a book in a long time.

9. A. Mom, who was the sixteenth president of the United States?

   B. I'm not sure. ______________________ American history in a long time.

10. A. Everyone says the new movie at the Center Cinema is excellent.

    B. Let's see it. We ________________ a good movie in a long time.

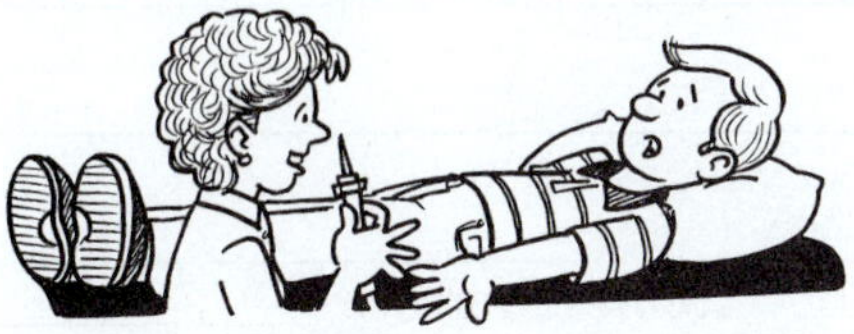

11. A. Are you nervous?

    B. Yes, I am. _________________________ blood in a long time.

12. A. What's Dad doing?

    B. He's making dinner. _______________ dinner in a long time.

13. A. Is there any fruit in the refrigerator?

    B. No, there isn't. I __________________ to the supermarket in a long time.

14. A. Ouch!!

    B. Sorry. ____________________________ in a long time.

M PUZZLE: *What Have They Already Done?*

Across

1. wash
5. fly
8. go
10. explain
11. meet
12. take

Down

2. see
3. drive
4. play
6. wear
7. drink
8. get
9. be

N A LOT OF THINGS TO DO

Richard is going to have a party tonight, and he has a lot of things to do.

- ✔ go to the supermarket
- ☐ clean my apartment
- ✔ get a haircut
- ☐ bake a cake
- ✔ fix my CD player

1. He's already gone to the supermarket.
2. He hasn't cleaned his apartment yet.
3. ______________________
4. ______________________
5. ______________________

Susan is going to work this morning, and she has a lot of things to do.

- ✔ take a shower
- ☐ do my exercises
- ☐ feed the cat
- ✔ walk the dog
- ☐ eat breakfast

6. ______________________
7. ______________________
8. ______________________
9. ______________________
10. ______________________

Beverly and Paul are going on a trip tomorrow, and they have a lot of things to do.

- ☐ do our laundry
- ✔ get our paychecks
- ✔ pay our bills
- ☐ pack our suitcases
- ☐ say good-bye to our friends

11. ______________________
12. ______________________
13. ______________________
14. ______________________
15. ______________________

Roberta is very busy today. She has a lot of things to do at the office.

- [x] write to Mrs. Lane
- [x] call Mr. Sanchez
- [ ] meet with Ms. Wong
- [ ] read my e-mail
- [x] send a fax to the Ace Company

16. ______________________________
17. ______________________________
18. ______________________________
19. ______________________________
20. ______________________________

You have a lot of things to do today. What have you done? What haven't you done?

1. ....
2. ....
3. ....
4. ....
5. ....

O LISTENING

What things have these people done? What haven't they done? Listen and check *Yes* or *No*.

		Yes	*No*			*Yes*	*No*
1.	do homework	✔	____	5.	do the laundry	____	____
	practice the violin	____	✔		vacuum the rugs	____	____
2.	write the report	____	____	6.	get the food	____	____
	send a fax	____	____		clean the house	____	____
3.	feed the dog	____	____	7.	speak to the landlord	____	____
	eat breakfast	____	____		call Ajax Electric	____	____
4.	fix the pipes	____	____	8.	hook up the VCR	____	____
	repair the washing machine	____	____		read the instructions	____	____

P WHAT ARE THEY SAYING?

1. A. Have you spoken to David recently?

B. Yes, I have. I __________ to him last night.

A. What ________ he say?

B. He's worried because he's going to fly in a helicopter this week, and he's never __________ in a helicopter before.

2. A. __________ you seen any good movies recently?

B. No, I __________. I __________ a movie last week, but it was terrible.

A. Really? What movie did you ________?

B. *The Man from Madagascar.* It's one of the worst movies I've ever __________.

3. A. I think I forgot to do something, but I can't remember what I forgot to do.

B. Have you __________ the mail to the post office?

A. Yes. I ________ it to the post office an hour ago.

B. __________ you __________ a fax to the Ace Company?

A. Yes. I __________ them a fax this morning.

B. __________ you __________ the employees their paychecks?

A. Uh-oh! That's what I forgot to do!

4. A. __________ you gone on vacation yet?

B. Yes, I __________. I __________ to Venice. It was phenomenal!

A. __________ you ever __________ to Venice before?

B. Yes, I __________. I __________ there a few years ago.

5. A. What _______ you get for your birthday?

B. My family __________ me seventy-five dollars.

A. That's fantastic! What _________________________?

B. Going to buy? I've already ____________ all my birthday money.

A. Really? What ________________ buy?

B. I ______________ a lot of CDs. Do you want to ____________ to them?

6. A. Are you ready to leave soon?

B. No, ____________. I haven't ____________ a shower yet.

A. But you __________ up an hour ago. You're really slow today. __________ you eaten breakfast yet?

B. Of course __________. I ______ a little while ago, and I've already ______________ the dishes.

A. Well, hurry up! It's 8:30. I don't want to be late.

Q LISTENING

Listen to each word and then say it.

1. job
2. jacket
3. juice
4. jam
5. jog
6. pajamas
7. journalist
8. just
9. Jennifer
10. you
11. yoga
12. yellow
13. yard
14. yesterday
15. young
16. yogurt
17. yet
18. New York

R JULIA'S BROKEN KEYBOARD

Julia's keyboard is broken. The j's and the y's don't always work. Fill in the missing j's and y's and then read Julia's letters aloud.

1.

Judy,

Have you seen my blue and yellow jacket at ___our house? I think I left it there ___esterday after the ___azz concert. I've looked everywhere, and I ___ust can't find it anywhere.

___ulia

2.

Dear ___ennifer,

We're sorry ___ou haven't been able to visit us this ___ear. Do ___ou think ___ou could come in ___une or ___uly? We really en___oyed ___our visit last ___ear. We really want to see ___ou again.

___ulia

3.

___eff,

___ack and I have gone out ___ogging, but we'll be back in ___ust a few minutes. Make ___ourself comfortable. ___ou can wait for us in the ___ard. We haven't eaten lunch ___et. We'll have some ___ogurt and orange ___uice when we get back.

___ulia

4.

Dear ___ane,

We ___ust received the beautiful pa___amas ___ou sent to ___immy. Thank ___ou very much. ___immy is too ___oung to write to ___ou himself, but he says "Thank ___ou." He's already worn the pa___amas, and he's en___oying them a lot.

___ulia

5.

Dear ___anet,

___ack and I are coming to visit ___ou and ___ohn in New ___ork. We've been to New ___ork before, but we haven't visited the Statue of Liberty or the Empire State Building ___et. See ___ou in ___anuary or maybe in ___une.

___ulia

6.

Dear ___oe,

We got a letter from ___ames last week. He has en___oyed college a lot this ___ear. His favorite sub___ects are German and ___apanese. He's looking for a ___ob as a ___ournalist in ___apan, but he hasn't found one ___et.

___ulia

S IS OR HAS?

1. He's already eaten lunch.
   ______ is
   ___✔___ has

2. He's eating lunch.
   ___✔___ is
   ______ has

3. She's taking a bath.
   ______ is
   ______ has

4. She's taken a bath.
   ______ is
   ______ has

5. He's having a good time.
   ______ is
   ______ has

6. She's going to get up.
   ______ is
   ______ has

7. He's bought a lot of CDs recently.
   ______ is
   ______ has

8. It's snowing.
   ______ is
   ______ has

9. She's thirsty.
   ______ is
   ______ has

10. He's got to leave now.
    ______ is
    ______ has

11. Where's the nearest health club?
    ______ is
    ______ has

12. She's written the report.
    ______ is
    ______ has

13. He's taking a lot of photographs.
    ______ is
    ______ has

14. He's taken a few photographs.
    ______ is
    ______ has

15. He's spent all his money.
    ______ is
    ______ has

16. There's a library across the street.
    ______ is
    ______ has

17. She's gone kayaking.
    ______ is
    ______ has

18. It's very warm.
    ______ is
    ______ has

19. He's embarrassed.
    ______ is
    ______ has

20. This is the best book she's ever read.
    ______ is
    ______ has

A HOW LONG?

for since

1.

2. How long have your parents been married?

____ a long time.

3. How long has your brother owned a motorcycle?

____ last summer.

4. How long has your sister been interested in astronomy?

____ several years.

5. How long have you had a cell phone?

____ last month.

6. How long have you and your husband known each other?

____ 1994.

7. How long have the Wilsons had a dog?

____ a few weeks.

8. How long have you had problems with your upstairs neighbor?

____ a year.

9. How long has your daughter been a computer programmer?

____ 2000.

10. How long has your son played in the school orchestra?

____ September.

11. How long have there been mice in your attic?

____ two months.

B WHAT'S THE QUESTION?

1. How long has your daughter wanted to be an engineer?

   She's wanted to be an engineer for a long time.

2. ______________ James ______________?

   He's owned his own house since 2001.

3. ______________ your grandparents ______________?

   They've been married for 50 years.

4. ______________ you ______________?

   I've been interested in photography since last year.

5. ______________ Gregory ______________?

   He's worn glasses since last spring.

6. ______________ your cousins ______________?

   They've known how to snowboard for a few years.

7. ______________ your son ______________?

   He's had a girlfriend for several months.

8. ______________ there ______________?

   There's been a pizza shop in town since last fall.

C GrammarRap: *How Long Have You Known Maria?*

Listen. Then clap and practice.

A. How long have you known Maria?
B. I've known her since I was two.
A. Have you met her older sister?
B. No, I haven't. Have you?

A. How long has your son been in college?
B. He's been there since early September.
A. Does he like all of his courses?
B. I think so. I can't remember.

A. How long have your friends lived in London?
B. They've lived there since two thousand one.
A. Have you visited them since they moved there?
B. Yes, I have. It was fun.

A. How long has your brother been married?
B. He's been married for seven months.
A. Have you seen him since his wedding?
B. I've seen him only once.

D SINCE WHEN?

1. ___I'm___ sick today.

___I've been sick___ since I got up this morning.

2. Rita __________ a swollen knee.

__________________ a swollen knee since she played soccer last Saturday.

3. Roger __________ how to ski.

__________________ how to ski since he took lessons last winter.

4. ________ nervous.

__________________ nervous since they got married a few hours ago.

5. __________ lost.

__________________ lost since we arrived here this morning.

6. I __________ a stiff neck.

__________________ a stiff neck since I went to a tennis match yesterday.

7. __________ cold and cloudy.

__________________ cold and cloudy since we got here last weekend.

8. My daughter __________ the cello.

__________ played the cello since she was six years old.

9. My boyfriend __________ bored.

__________________ bored since the concert began forty-five minutes ago.

10. __________ afraid of dogs.

__________________ afraid of dogs since my neighbor's dog bit me last year.

E LISTENING

Listen and choose the correct answer.

1. a. Bob is in the army.
   (b.) Bob is engaged.
2. a. Carol is in music school.
   b. Carol is a professional musician.
3. a. Michael has been home for a week.
   b. Michael hurt himself this week.
4. a. She hasn't started her new job.
   b. She gets up early every morning.
5. a. Richard is in college.
   b. Richard hasn't eaten in the cafeteria.
6. a. Nancy and Tom met five and a half years ago.
   b. Nancy and Tom met when they were five and a half years old.
7. a. They play soccer every weekend.
   b. They're eight years old.
8. a. Patty is a teenager.
   b. Patty has short hair.
9. a. Ron used to own his own business.
   b. Ron moved nine years ago.
10. a. She's interested in astronomy.
    b. She's eleven years old.
11. a. He's in high school.
    b. He isn't in high school now.
12. a. Alan has owned his house for fifteen years.
    b. Alan doesn't have problems with his house now.

F CROSSWORD

dizzy	fever	measles	nauseous	sore	stiff

Across

3. My throat has been very ______ since Tuesday.
4. I haven't been able to eat since yesterday. I feel ______.
6. I've had a ______ neck for a week.

Down

1. I've had a high ______ for 24 hours.
2. My children have had little red spots all over their bodies for two days. They have the ______.
5. I've been ______ since I fell down and hurt my head.

G SCRAMBLED SENTENCES

Unscramble the sentences.

1. she a jazz Julie liked teenager. has was since

   Julie has liked jazz since she was a teenager.

2. he play little the since known a boy. He's piano was how to

   ______

3. since I've was in I astronomy young. interested been

   ______

4. since been they college. engaged They've finished

   ______

5. been he a cooking He's graduated from chef school. since

   ______

6. she wanted be to teacher eighteen She's a years since old. was

   ______

7. moved ago. business They've their year owned since a they here own

   ______

H WRITE ABOUT YOURSELF

1. I'm interested in ______.

   I've been interested in ______ since ______.

2. I own ______.

   I've owned ______ since ______.

3. I like ______.

   I've ______ since ______.

4. I want to ______.

   I've ______ since ______.

5. I know how to ______.

   I've ______ since ______.

I THEN AND NOW

be   have   speak   teach   visit   walk

1. Mr. and Mrs. Miller __walk__ every day. ____________ every day since Mr. Miller had problems with his heart last year. Before that, ____________ never ________. They stayed home and watched TV.

2. Sam ____________ with a Boston accent. ____________ with a Boston accent since he moved to Boston last summer. Before that, ____________ with a New York accent.

3. Terry ________ a truck driver. She drives a truck between the east coast and the west coast. ____________ a truck driver for a year. Before that, ____________ a taxi driver.

4. Before he moved to Brazil, Professor Baker ________ French. Now ____________ English. ____________ English at a Brazilian university for the past two years.

5. Your Uncle Walter ________ already ____________ us five times this year! Last year, he ____________ us only twice. How many times will he ________ us next year?!

6. Tiffany ________ long blond hair. ____________ long blond hair since she became a movie star. Before that, she ________ short brown hair. Tiffany looks very different now!

J LOOKING BACK

Victor
(be)
musician 1990–now
photographer 1982–1989

1. How long has Victor been a musician?
He's been a musician since 1990.

2. How long was he a photographer?
He was a photographer for 7 years.

Mrs. Sanchez
(teach)
science 1995–now
math 1985–1994

3. How long ________ science?
________ since ________.

4. How long ________ math?
________ for ________.

my grandparents
(have)
dog 1998–now
cat 1986–1997

5. How long ________ a cat?
________ for ________.

6. How long ________ a dog?
________ since ________.

Betty
(work)
bank 2000–now
mall 1997–1999

7. How long ________ at the bank?
________ since ________.

8. How long ________ at the mall?
________ for ________.

my parents
(live)
Miami 2001–now
New York 1980–2000

9. How long ________ in New York?
________ for ________.

10. How long ________ in Miami?
________ since ________.

K HIGH SCHOOL REUNION

1. Do you still go skiing every winter?

No. ....
.... (for/since) ....
....

2. Do you still live ....
.... ?

No. ....
.... (for/since) ....
....

3. Are you still a/an ....
.... ?

No. ....
.... (for/since) ....
....

4. How long have you been interested in
.... ?

....
.... (for/since) ....
....

5. Do you still ....
....
in your free time?

No. ....
.... (for/since) ....
....

6. Do your brothers still call you "Tiny Tim"?

No. ______________________________

______________ (for/since) ______________

______________________________.

7. How long have you ______________

____

______________________________?

____

______________ (for/since) ______________

______________________________.

8. Do you still ______________

____

______________________________?

No. ______________________________

______________ (for/since) ______________

______________________________.

L LISTENING

Listen and choose the correct answer.

1. a. He's always been a salesperson.
   (b.) He was a cashier.
2. a. His daughter was in medical school.
   b. His daughter is in medical school.
3. a. Her parents haven't always lived in a house.
   b. Her parents have always lived in a house.
4. a. He's always wanted to be an actor.
   b. He isn't in college now.
5. a. They exercise at their health club every day.
   b. They haven't exercised at their health club since last year.
6. a. James hasn't always been a bachelor.
   b. James has been married for ten years.
7. a. Jane has wanted to meet a writer.
   b. Jane wants to be a writer.
8. a. He's never broken his ankle.
   b. He's never sprained his ankle.
9. a. She's always liked rock music.
   b. She hasn't always liked classical music.
10. a. Billy has had a fever for two days.
    b. Billy has had a sore throat for two days.
11. a. Jennifer has always been the manager.
    b. Jennifer hasn't been a salesperson since last fall.
12. a. He's interested in modern art now.
    b. He's always been interested in art.

6

A WHAT'S THE WORD?

for	since

1. We've been living here __since__ 2001.

2. It's been raining ________ two days.

3. I've been listening to this CD ________ an hour.

4. She's been flying airplanes ________ 1995.

5. Billy, you've been roller-blading ________ this morning!

6. He's been practicing the cello ________ three and a half hours.

7. Our neighbors have been vacuuming ________ 7 A.M.

8. We've been having problems with our heat ________ a week.

B CHOOSE

1. I've been working here since ______.
   (a.) last month
   b. three months

2. He's been taking a shower for ______.
   a. this afternoon
   b. half an hour

3. It's been ringing for ______.
   a. two o'clock
   b. a few minutes

4. She's been studying since ______.
   a. eight o'clock
   b. an hour

5. They've been dating for ______.
   a. high school
   b. six months

6. I've been feeling sick since ______.
   a. twelve hours
   b. yesterday

C HOW LONG?

1. How long have you been studying?

I've been studying since early this morning.

2. How long has Ann been feeling sick?

______________________ a few days.

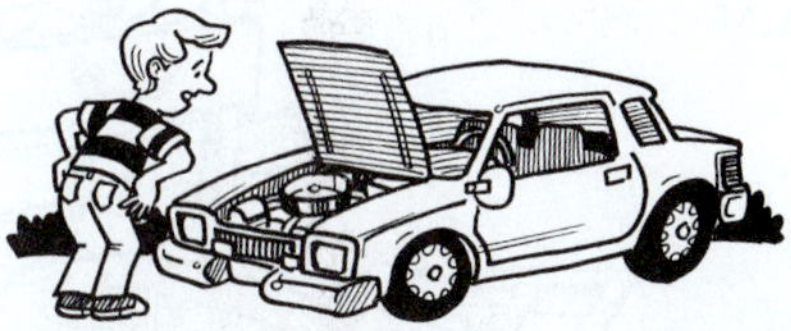

3. How long has Tom been having problems with his car?

______________________ a week.

4. How long have the people next door been arguing?

______________________ last night.

5. How long have we been waiting?

______________________ forty-five minutes.

6. How long has that cell phone been ringing?

______________________ the play began.

7. How long has Professor Drake been talking?

______________________ an hour and a half.

8. How long have Rick and Sally been dating?

______________________ high school.

9. How long have you been teaching?

______________________ 1975.

10. How long have I been chatting online?

______________________ more than two hours.

D WHAT ARE THEY DOING?

assemble	bake	bark	browse	do	jog	look	make	plant

1. Larry ___is looking___ for his keys.
   ___He's been looking___ for his keys all morning.
2. My sister ________ in the park.
   ________________ in the park since 8 A.M.
3. The dog next door ________.
   ________________ all day.
4. Our neighbors ________ flowers.
   ________________ flowers for several hours.
5. Michael ________ his homework.
   ________________ his homework since dinner.
6. My wife ________ the web.
   ________________ the web for an hour.
7. Mr. and Mrs. Lee ________ their son's new bicycle.
   ________________ it all afternoon.
8. I'm ________ cookies.
   ________________ cookies since two o'clock.
9. You and your brother ________ a lot of noise!
   ________________ noise since you got up.

E LISTENING

Listen and choose the correct time expressions to complete the sentences.

1. (a.) 1995.
   b. a few years.
2. a. 1:45.
   b. forty-five minutes.
3. a. 3 o'clock.
   b. thirty minutes.
4. a. yesterday.
   b. several days.
5. a. 7:30 this morning.
   b. more than an hour.
6. a. 7 o'clock.
   b. a half hour.
7. a. a few weeks.
   b. last month.
8. a. about three hours.
   b. 4 o'clock.
9. a. early this morning.
   b. twenty minutes.

F GrammarRap: *How Long?*

Listen. Then clap and practice.

A. How long have you been working at the mall?

B. I've been working at the mall since the fall.

A. How long has she been wearing her new ring?

B. She's been wearing her new ring since the spring.

A. How long have you been living in L.A.?

B. We've been living in L.A. since May.

A. How long has he been waiting for the train?

B. He's been waiting since it started to rain.

A. How long have you been looking for that mouse?

B. We've been looking since we rented this house.

G WHAT ARE THEY SAYING?

make	play	run	snow	study	take	vacuum	wait	wear	work

1. Excuse me. Have you been waiting in line for a long time?

Yes, I have. I've been waiting for more than an hour.

2. What a terrible day! ______________ for a long time?

Yes, ______________. ______________ since early this morning.

3. Your son plays the violin very beautifully. ______________ lessons for a long time?

Yes, ______________. ______________ lessons since he was five.

4. ______________ here for a long time?

No, ______________. I've ______________ here for only a week.

5. __________ your car ______________ strange noises for a long time?

Yes, ______________. ______________ these noises all week.

6. You look tired. ______________ for a long time?

Yes, ______________. ______________ all morning.

7. Your children speak French very well.
______ it for a long time?

Yes, ______.
______ French for six years.

8. I'm really tired.
______ for a long time?

Yes, we ______.
______ since 6 A.M.

9. Your pants are dirty.
______ them all week?

No, ______.
______ them for only a few hours.

10. This is the sixth game you've won today.
______ for a long time?

No, ______.
______ for only a few months.

H LISTENING

Listen and choose what the people are talking about.

1. (a.) traffic
   b. a computer
2. a. a wall
   b. the furniture
3. a. the guitar
   b. my bills
4. a. the drums
   b. tennis
5. a. the cookies
   b. the babies
6. a. the cake
   b. the bridge
7. a. her composition
   b. her bicycle
8. a. books
   b. trains
9. a. a sandwich
   b. a novel
10. a. socks
    b. chairs
11. a. the president
    b. CDs
12. a. a restaurant
    b. a neighbor
13. a. fruit
    b. my car
14. a. a test
    b. a cake
15. a. videos
    b. problems

I SOUND IT OUT!

Listen to each word and then say it.

this

1. bills	3. chicken	5. building
2. officer	4. ticket	6. itself

these

1. week	3. briefcase	5. fever
2. speak	4. friendly	6. eaten

Listen and put a circle around the word that has the same sound.

1. thin:	police	tired	interested
2. build:	headache	is	sweater
3. read:	Steve's	been	try
4. if:	in	bite	taxi
5. live:	met	history	child
6. fishing:	science	writing	sister
7. piece:	very	wear	winter
8. east:	hire	Chinese	ready

Now make a sentence using all the words you circled, and read the sentence aloud.

9. ....

10. key:	dinner	receive	think
11. tennis:	easy	heater	this
12. complete:	any	get	try
13. keep:	busy	Peter	disturb
14. tuxedo:	type	if	week
15. Linda:	didn't	green	bright
16. meeting:	child	forget	e-mail

Now make a sentence using all the words you circled, and read the sentence aloud.

17. ....

J YOU DECIDE: *What Have They Been Doing?*

1. 

I have a sore throat.

No wonder you have a sore throat!

You've been singing all day.

2. 

My back hurts.

No wonder your back hurts!

.... all day.

3. 

Bob has a terrible sunburn.

No wonder he has a terrible sunburn!

.... all day.

4. 

Nancy is very tired.

No wonder she's very tired!

.... all day.

5. 

Jane and I have headaches.

No wonder you have headaches!

.... all day.

6. 

Bob and Judy are very disappointed.

No wonder they're very disappointed!

.... all day.

7. 

I can't finish my dinner.

No wonder you can't finish your dinner!

.... all day.

8. 

Victor doesn't have any money.

No wonder he doesn't have any money!

.... all day.

K WHAT'S HAPPENING?

complain	eat	go	make	read	see	study	swim	talk	write

1. 

My husband and I are very full. ___We've been eating___ for the past two hours. ___We've___ already ___eaten___ soup, salad, chicken, and vegetables. And our dinner isn't finished. ___We haven't eaten___ our dessert yet!

2. 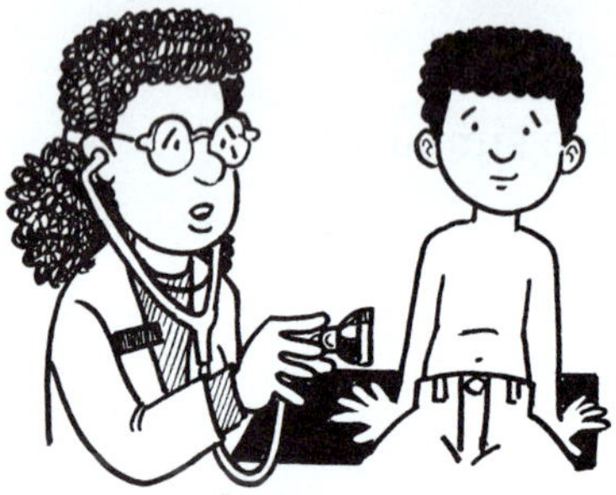

Dr. Davis is tired. ______________ patients since early this morning. ________ already ______________ twenty patients, and it's only two o'clock. ______________ the other patients in her waiting room yet.

3. 

Dave likes to swim. ______________ for an hour and a half. ________ already ______________ across the pool thirty times.

4. 

Amy is very tired. ______________ to job interviews for the past three weeks. ________ already ______________ to ten job interviews, and she hasn't found a job yet!

5. 

Gregory loves to talk. ______________ all evening. ________ already ______________ about his job, his house, and his car. Fortunately, ______________ about his cats yet.

6. 

Betty and Bob are writing thank-you notes for their wedding gifts, and they're very tired. ______________ them all weekend. ________ already ______________ to their aunts, uncles, and cousins, but ______________ to their friends yet.

7. 

Andrew is tired. He's having a party tonight, and ____________ ____________ desserts since early this morning. ________ already ____________ two apple pies and three blueberry pies. But he isn't finished. ____________ a chocolate cake yet.

8. 

Patty is very tired. ____________ since she got home from school. ________ already ____________ English and math. And she'll be up late tonight because ____________ for her history test yet.

9. 

Today is Howard's day off, and he's enjoying himself. ________ ____________ since early this morning. ________ already ____________ three short stories. But ____________ today's newspaper yet.

10. 

Mr. and Mrs. Grumble like to complain. ____________ all evening. ________ already ____________ about their jobs, the weather, and several members of their family. Fortunately, they ____________ about the party yet, but I'm sure they will.

L LISTENING

Listen and decide where the conversation is taking place.

1. (a.) in a kitchen
   b. in a supermarket
2. a. at home
   b. in school
3. a. in a department store
   b. in a laundromat
4. a. at a movie theater
   b. at home
5. a. at a clinic
   b. at a bakery
6. a. in a cafeteria
   b. in a library
7. a. at a concert hall
   b. at a museum
8. a. at a health club
   b. in a book store
9. a. in an office
   b. at a bus stop
10. a. at a zoo
    b. in a pet shop
11. a. at home
    b. at a movie theater
12. a. at a clinic
    b. in a department store

M WHICH WORD?

1. The floor is wet! How long has the ceiling been [leaking / leaked] ?

2. I'm not nervous. I've been [flown / flying] in helicopters for years.

3. I'm a little worried. I've never [been running / run] in a marathon before.

4. How many pizzas have you already [made / been making] so far today?

5. You look tired. What [have you / have you been] doing today?

6. I think I've [seen / been seeing] this movie before.

7. Has your husband already [giving / given] blood?

8. I've never [taken / been taking] a karate lesson. Have you?

9. Have you ever [been going / gone] out on a date before?

10. Alexander, your cell phone [has rung / has been ringing] since we started class!

11. Jane isn't nervous. She's been [sung / singing] in front of audiences for years.

N YOU DECIDE: *What Are They Saying?*

A. Mrs. Vickers, could I speak to you for a few minutes?

B. Of course. Please sit down.

A. Mrs. Vickers, I've been thinking. I've been working here at the

________ Company (for/since) ________.
I've worked very hard, and I've done a lot of things here.

For example, I've ________,

I've ________,

and I've been ________

(for/since) ________.

B. That's true, Mr. Mills. And we're happy with your work.

A. Thank you, Mrs. Vickers. As I was saying, I know I've done a very good job here, and I really think I should get a raise.

I haven't had a raise (for/since) ________.

B. ________.

A. ________.

A. Dad, could I speak to you for a few minutes?

B. Sure, James. Please sit down.

A. Dad, I've been thinking. I've been working very hard in school this year, and I've done all my chores at home. For example,

I've ________, I've ________

________, and I've been ________

________ (for/since) ________.

B. That's true, James. Your mother and I are very proud of you.

A. Thank you, Dad. As I was saying, I know I've been very responsible, and I really think I should be able to take your car when I go out on a date. After all, I've been driving

(for/since) ________.

B. ________.

A. ________.

O A NEW LIFE

Daniel has been living in a small town in Mexico all his life. His father just got a good job in the United States, and Daniel and his family are going to live there. Daniel's life is going to be very different in the United States.

1. He's going to live in a big city.
2. He's going to take English lessons.
3. He's going to take the subway.
4. He's going to shop in American supermarkets.
5. He's going to eat American food.
6. He's going to play American football.
7. He's going to ______.

Daniel is a little nervous.

1. He's never lived in a big city before.
2. ______ before.
3. ______ before.
4. ______ before.
5. ______ before.
6. ______ before.
7. ______ before.

Daniel's cousins have been living in the United States for many years. They'll be able to help him.

8. They've been living in a big city for years.
9. ______ for years.
10. ______ for years.
11. ______ for years.
12. ______ for years.
13. ______ for years.
14. ______ for years.

Daniel's cousins tell him he shouldn't worry. They're sure he'll enjoy his new life in the United States very much.

P YOU DECIDE: *A New Life*

.... has been living in ....

all her life. Now she's going to move to .... (your city).

Her life is going to be very different in .... (your city).

1. She's going to ....
2. She's going to ....
3. She's going to ....
4. She's going to ....
5. She's going to ....

____________ is a little nervous.

6. ____________ before.
7. ____________ before.
8. ____________ before.
9. ____________ before.
10. ____________ before.

.... (has/have) been living in ____________ for many years and will be able to help her.

11. ____________ for years.
12. ____________ for years.
13. ____________ for years.
14. ____________ for years.
15. ____________ for years.

____________ shouldn't worry. I'm sure she'll enjoy her new life in ____________ very much.

✓ CHECK-UP TEST: Chapters 4–6

A. Complete the sentences with the present perfect.

Ex. *(do)* Julie ___has___ already ___done___ her homework.

(read) I ___haven't read___ your report yet.

(eat) 1. Mary and her brother __________ already ______________ breakfast.

(take) 2. My nephew ____________________ his violin lesson yet.

(write) 3. I ______________________________ to my grandparents yet.

(go) 4. My wife __________ already ______________ to work.

(pay) 5. You ________________________ your electric bill yet.

(have) 6. Henry __________ already ______________ a problem with his new cell phone.

B. Complete the questions.

1. A. ______________________ to your supervisor yet?
   B. Yes, I have. I spoke to her this morning.

2. A. ___________________ his new bicycle yet?
   B. Yes, he has. He rode it this morning.

3. A. ___________________ their paychecks yet?
   B. Yes, they have. They got them this afternoon.

4. A. ____________ ever ____________ in a helicopter?
   B. Yes, he has. He flew in a helicopter last summer.

5. A. ____________ ever __________ on TV?
   B. Yes, she has. She was on TV last week.

6. A. __________________ your daughter's new boyfriend yet?
   B. No, I haven't. I'm going to meet him tonight.

C. Complete the sentences.

Ex. My neck is very stiff. ___It's been___ stiff since I got up this morning.

Tom is reading his e-mail. ___He's been reading___ it for a half hour.

1. It's sunny. ________________________ all week.
2. We're browsing the web. ________________________________ the web since 8 o'clock.
3. My daughter has a fever. ________________________ a fever since early this morning.
4. My son is studying. ________________________ since he got home from school.
5. Our neighbors are arguing. ________________________________ all afternoon.
6. I know how to skate. ________________________ how to skate since I was six years old.

7. Susan is interested in science. ______________ interested in science since she was a teenager.

8. My husband and I are cleaning our basement. __________________________ it all weekend.

D. Complete the answers.

for	since

1. How long has your wife been working at the bank?

   ____ 1999.

2. How long have those dogs been barking?

   ____ a long time.

3. How long has it been snowing?

   ____ two days.

4. How long have you wanted to be an astronaut?

   ____ I was six years old.

E. Complete the sentences.

1. My brother owns a motorcycle. ____________________ a motorcycle since last summer.

   Before that, ________________ a bicycle.

2. I'm a journalist. ________________ a journalist since 2000.

   Before that, ________________ an actor.

3. My daughter likes classical music. ______________________ classical music since she finished college.

   Before that, ________________ rock music.

F. Listen and choose the correct answer.

1. a. Janet is in acting school.
   b. Janet is an actress.

2. a. The president has finished his speech.
   b. The president is still speaking.

3. a. They've been living in New York since 1995.
   b. They haven't lived in New York since 1995.

4. a. They're going to eat later.
   b. They're going to eat now.

5. a. She's called the superintendent.
   b. She has to call the superintendent.

6. a. Someone is helping Billy with his homework.
   b. No one is helping Billy with his homework.

A WHAT DO THEY {ENJOY DOING / LIKE TO DO}?

enjoy ________ing	like to ________	________ing

1. My wife and I ___enjoy___ relaxing on the beach when we go on vacation.

2. Mrs. Finn is very talkative. She ___likes to___ talk about her grandchildren.

   ___Talking___ about her grandchildren is important to her.

3. Billy doesn't ____________ going to the doctor, but he went yesterday for his annual checkup.

4. I ____________ knit sweaters. ________________ sweaters is a good way to relax.

5. My husband doesn't ______________ asking for a raise, but sometimes he has to.

6. Dr. Brown ______________ deliver babies. In her opinion, ________________ babies is the best job in the world.

7. Bob doesn't ____________ being a bachelor. He thinks ______________ married is better.

8. Ann ____________ plant flowers. She thinks __________________ flowers is good exercise.

9. Jim ____________ chatting online with his friends, but his parents think ________________ online every evening isn't a very good idea.

10. Tom doesn't ______________ play hockey. He thinks ______________ hockey is dangerous.

11. My parents go to the gym during the winter, but in the summer they ____________ going hiking.

12. Martin ____________ go to parties. He thinks ____________ to parties is a good way to meet people.

13. I really want to play the piano well, but I don't ____________ practicing.

B GrammarRap: *Writing Is Fun*

Listen. Then clap and practice.

Writing is fun.
I like to write.
I enjoy writing letters late at night.

Eating is fun.
I like to eat.
I enjoy eating fish, and I like eating meat.

Skiing is great.
He likes to ski.
But skiing's been hard since he hurt his knee.

Singing is fun.
She likes to sing.
But today she's sick, and she can't sing a thing.

Running is great.
They like to run.
Swimming's okay, but running's more fun.

Baking is great.
He likes to bake.
When he's feeling sad, he bakes a cake.

Knitting is fun.
She likes to knit.
She enjoys knitting sweaters, but none of them fit!

C WHAT'S THE WORD?

clean	complain	eat	go	sit	wear
cleaning	complaining	eating	going	sitting	wearing

1. I hate to ___complain___, but your loud music is disturbing me.
2. Carol tries to avoid ______________ in the sun.
3. Sally likes to ______________ dinner at home.
4. My son hates to ______________ his room.
5. Richard can't stand to ______________ a tie.
6. Tom avoids ______________ his apartment whenever he can.
7. James doesn't like to ______________ to the mall.
8. My husband and I hate ______________ sailing.
9. My wife and I like to ______________ in the park on a sunny day.
10. Please try to avoid ______________ about the weather all the time.
11. My friends and I can't stand ______________ in fast-food restaurants.
12. My daughter likes ______________ the sweater you gave her for her birthday.

D GRAMMARRAP: *Pet Peeves*

Listen. Then clap and practice.

I don't like waiting for the bus in the rain.
I hate to rush when I'm late for a plane.
I avoid talking to strangers on the train.
I can't stand driving in the center lane.

I don't like to iron on a hot summer day.
I hate to clean the house in the middle of May.
I avoid dusting and sweeping my floors.
I can't stand doing all my household chores!

E YOU DECIDE: *What's the Reason?*

1. David is happy he works in a gym because he enjoys

exercising every day.

2. Gloria hates being a taxi driver because she can't stand

....

3. Miguel is glad he lives in Puerto Rico because he likes

....

4. I'm sorry I'm a secretary because I can't stand

....

5. We're happy we're going camping because we enjoy

....

6. William is upset he's sick because he hates

....

7. I'm glad I have a new bicycle because I like

....

8. Norman doesn't like being on a diet because he can't stand

....

9. Julie is happy she's a Hollywood actress because she enjoys

....

F MY ENERGETIC GRANDFATHER

A. Your grandfather is very energetic!

B. He sure is!

A. When did he start ______ [1] the drums?

B. Believe it or not, he learned ______ [2] the drums when he was sixty years old!

A. That's incredible! Does he ______ [3] the drums often?

B. Yes, he does. He's played every day for the last eight years.

A. What else does he enjoy doing?

B. He enjoys ______ [4], he enjoys ______ [5], and he also enjoys ______ [6].

A. I hope I have that much energy when I'm his age!

G I CAN'T STAND IT!

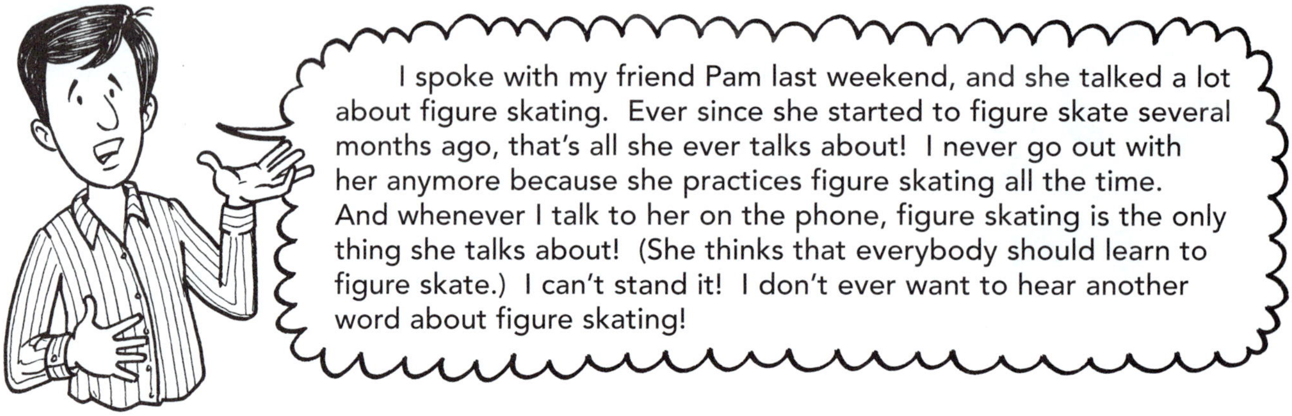

Now YOU tell about somebody.

I spoke to my friend ______ last weekend, and ______ talked a lot about ______. Ever since ______

______

______

______

______

______.

H CHOOSE

1. I've decided [buy / buying / (to buy)] a motorcycle.

2. Have you ever considered [to move / moving / move] ?

3. I'm thinking about [going / to go / go] on a diet.

4. You should consider [to change / change / changing] jobs.

5. Have you decided to [get / to get / getting] a dog?

6. He's thought about [to retire / retiring / retire] .

I GrammarRap: *I Considered Ordering the Cheesecake*

Listen. Then clap and practice.

I considered ordering the cheesecake.
Everyone said I should try it.
But then I decided to skip dessert.
I wanted to stay on my diet.

I thought about going home early.
It was only a quarter to ten.
But I changed my mind and decided to stay
When the music started again.

I thought about moving to France
And studying music and dance.
But I changed my mind and decided to stay
With my cat and my bird and my plants.

J YOU DECIDE: *What's Carla Going to Do?*

A. Hi, Carla. How are you? We haven't spoken in a long time. Tell me, what have you been doing?

B. ....

A. Oh. And what are you thinking about doing after you finish studying English?

B. For a while, I considered .... ,

and then I thought about ....

But I finally decided to ....

A. Oh. Why did you decide to do that?

B. Because ....

A. That's interesting. Tell me, Carla, have you ever considered ....

.... ?

B. Yes. I thought about doing that, but decided it wasn't a very good idea.

A. Why not?

B. Because ....

A. Oh, I see.

B. So, Kathy, do you think I'm making the right decision?

A. ....

B. Do you really think so?

A. ....

B. Well, it was great talking to you. Let's get together soon.

A. Okay. I'll call you and we'll make some plans.

K WHAT'S THE WORD?

1. You can't keep on __rearranging__ the furniture so often. You rearranged it last weekend!
2. I stopped ______________ meat. I only eat fish and chicken.
3. He tried to quit ________________, but he couldn't. He still worries about everything.
4. Alice always gets up late. She should start ______________ up earlier.
5. Richard doesn't exercise very often. He should begin ________________ every day. He'll feel a lot better.
6. You can't continue ______________ me the same question. You've already asked me ten times!
7. I realize that I can't keep on ______________ with people. I'm never going to argue with anyone again!
8. I know that Dave takes piano lessons. When did he start ______________ guitar lessons?
9. You should stop ______________ your bills late and start ______________ them on time.
10. Professor Blaine is very boring. Students continue ______________ asleep in his classes.

L GOOD DECISIONS

bite	clean	cook	do	gossip	interrupt	make	pay

This year I'm going to break all my bad habits. First, I've decided to stop __biting__ [1] my nails. I've also started ______________ [2] exercises every day. I learned ______________ [3] when I was young, so I've decided to start ______________ [4] healthy meals. I'm also considering ______________ [5] my bills on time, and I'm thinking about ______________ [6] my apartment every week. I've also decided to stop ______________ [7] about other people and to stop ______________ [8] my friends while they're talking.

M PROBLEMS!

1. 

My husband can't stop ___falling___ asleep at the movies. Every time we go, he falls asleep. If he keeps on __________ asleep, I'll never go to a movie with him again.

2. 

I don't think I should continue __________ weights every day. I like __________ weights, but I'm afraid I might hurt my back if I keep on __________ them so often.

3. 

My older sister always teases me. Today I'm really mad! She began __________ me early this morning, and she hasn't stopped. If she keeps on __________ me, I'm going to cry. And I won't stop __________ until she stops __________ me!

4. 

My friend Albert has got to stop __________ so fast and start __________ more carefully. If he continues __________ fast, I'm sure he'll have a serious accident some day.

5. 

Mr. Perkins, when are you going to stop __________ so sloppily and start __________ more neatly? If you keep on __________ like that, I'm going to have to fire you.

6. 

My boyfriend is very clumsy. When we go dancing, he keeps on __________ on my feet. If he doesn't start __________ more gracefully, I'm going to stop __________ dancing with him.

N LISTENING

Listen and choose the correct answer.

1. (a.) delivering babies.
   b. fix broken legs.
2. a. eating junk food.
   b. to pay our bills late.
3. a. swimming.
   b. to play golf.
4. a. to tap dance.
   b. figure skating.
5. a. to work out at a health club every week.
   b. retiring.
6. a. taking karate lessons.
   b. mend my pants.
7. a. to go back to college?
   b. moving?
8. a. to argue with people.
   b. biting my nails.
9. a. teasing your sister?
   b. to go to bed so late?
10. a. eat fruits and vegetables.
    b. worrying about my health all the time.
11. a. stand in line.
    b. wearing a suit.
12. a. taking photographs?
    b. study the piano?
13. a. to assemble his VCR.
    b. clean his apartment.
14. a. studying engineering.
    b. teach a computer course.
15. a. to live at home.
    b. going to school for the rest of your life.

O WHAT DOES IT MEAN?

Choose the correct answer.

1. My wife is very dizzy.
   a. I'm glad to hear that.
   (b.) How long has she been feeling sick?
   c. I guess she has a lot of things to do.
2. Peter and Nancy are vegetarians.
   a. They've quit eating vegetables.
   b. They've stopped planting flowers.
   c. They've stopped eating meat.
3. Andrew avoids talking about politics.
   a. He doesn't like talking about politics.
   b. He enjoys talking about politics.
   c. He's learning to talk about politics.
4. Shirley has worked her way to the top.
   a. She's the tallest person in her family.
   b. She's the president of her company.
   c. She works on the top floor of her building.
5. The people across the street were furious.
   a. They were embarrassed.
   b. They were awkward.
   c. They were very angry.
6. What's your present occupation?
   a. What do you do now?
   b. What are you going to do?
   c. What did you do when you were young?
7. This is my father-in-law, Mr. Kramer.
   a. He just graduated from high school.
   b. He just retired.
   c. He's seventeen years old.
8. My mother is going to mend my socks.
   a. She's going to fix them.
   b. She's going to wash them.
   c. She's going to send them to my sister.
9. You should stop gossiping.
   a. You should stop interrupting people.
   b. You should stop bumping into people.
   c. You should stop talking about people.
10. I've decided to ask for a raise.
    a. You should speak to your landlord.
    b. You should speak to your boss.
    c. You should speak to your instructor.
11. Dr. Wu has a lot of patients.
    a. That's true. She never gets angry.
    b. I know. She's a very popular doctor.
    c. That's true. She never gets sick.
12. My Uncle Gino has an Italian accent.
    a. He bought it when he went to Italy.
    b. He wears it all the time.
    c. Everybody knows he's from Italy.

A BEFORE

8

1. Lisa didn't feel very well when she got up this morning because she *(eat)* ___had___ ___eaten___ a lot of candy before she went to bed.
2. My husband invited his boss for dinner last Friday night, and he forgot to tell me. Unfortunately, I *(get)* ________ already ____________ tickets for a concert.
3. Our friends didn't stop showing us pictures of their grandson all evening. They *(visit)* ________ just ____________ him the day before.
4. I wanted to drive to the mountains with my friends yesterday, but they *(drive)* ________ ____________ to the mountains the afternoon before.
5. Andrew wasn't very happy when I visited him yesterday. He *(cut)* ________ just ________ himself while he was cooking dinner.
6. Alice couldn't buy the new printer she wanted because she *(spend)* ________ ____________ all her money on her vacation.
7. When my son got home from his date last night, my wife and I *(go)* ________ already ____________ to sleep.
8. My children didn't want to eat pancakes for breakfast yesterday morning because I *(make)* ________ ____________ pancakes the morning before.
9. I didn't see a movie with my friends last weekend because I *(see)* ________ ____________ three movies the weekend before.
10. When I got up this morning, my wife *(leave)* ________ already ____________ for work.
11. Norman was upset when I saw him yesterday morning. He *(have)* ________ ____________ a big argument with his next-door neighbor the night before.
12. When I saw Jill today, she was very happy. Her boyfriend *(give)* ________ just ____________ her a beautiful bracelet for her birthday.
13. Tom couldn't lend me his dictionary the other day because he *(lose)* ________ ____________ it the week before.

B GRAMMARRAP: *Never Before*

Listen. Then clap and practice.

She felt very happy when she left the store.
She had never bought a computer before.

He looked very nervous when he knocked on the door.
He had never gone out on a date before.

She felt very weak, and her throat was sore.
She had never had the flu before.

He felt very proud when his guests asked for more.
He had never baked a pie before.

She felt very foolish when her food hit the floor.
She had never eaten with chopsticks before.

He looked very scared when it started to roar.
He had never been close to a lion before.

She was very annoyed when he started to snore.
He had never made so much noise before.

He was very surprised when he opened the drawer.
He had never seen so much money before.

C LATE FOR EVERYTHING

Gary Gray was very upset yesterday. He didn't get up until 9:00, and as a result, he was late for everything all day!

1. He got to the train station at 9:45. The train ___had___ already ___left___.

2. He drove to the office and arrived late for an important meeting.

   It ________ already ______________.

3. He got to the restaurant at 1:00 to meet his friend Janet for lunch. However, she ________ already ________ back to work.

4. He got to the bank at 3:15, but he was too late. It ________ already ____________.

5. He got to the bird-watching lecture at 4:15. It ________ already ____________.

6. He had made plans to get together with his friend Tom. But he didn't get to Tom's office until 5:00. His friend Tom ________ already ____________.

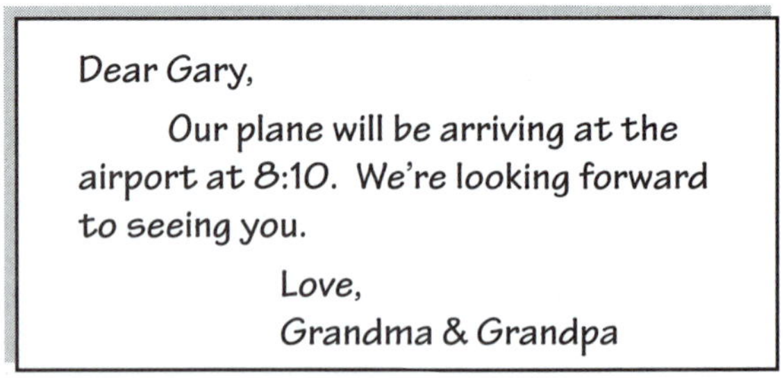

7. He drove to the airport to pick up his grandmother and grandfather. He got to the airport at 8:30. Their plane ________ already ______________.

D IN A LONG TIME

1. We got lost on the way to the party last night. We *(listen)* hadn't listened very carefully to the directions.

2. I enjoyed seeing my old friends at my high school reunion last weekend.

   I *(see)* __________ __________ them since we finished high school.

3. My wife and I decided to have a picnic in the park last Sunday. We *(have)* __________ __________ a picnic in the park in a long time.

4. I went dancing with my girlfriend last Saturday night, and I hurt my back.

   I *(go)* __________ __________ dancing in a long time.

5. Cynthia was embarrassed at her party last night. She had invited her cousin Charles, but she *(remember)* __________ __________ to invite his girlfriend, Louise.

6. Frank looked terrible when I saw him yesterday. His pants were dirty, he *(iron)* __________ __________ his shirt, and he *(shave)* __________ __________ in several days.

7. Michael was very discouraged when I saw him last week. He had been on a diet for a month, and he *(lose)* __________ __________ any weight.

8. Sylvia fell several times while she was skiing last weekend. She *(ski)* __________ __________ in a long time.

9. Arnold's boss fired him last week. Arnold *(get)* __________ __________ to work on time in six months.

10. Betty was very lucky she didn't miss her plane this morning. She got to the airport late, but the plane *(take off)* __________ __________ yet.

11. Alan did poorly on his English exam last week. I'm not surprised. He *(study)* __________ __________ for the test.

12. Stuart enjoyed riding his bicycle last weekend. He *(ride)* __________ __________ it in a long time.

E WORKING HARD

Jennifer was very busy after school yesterday.

1:00	write an English composition
2:00	study for my science test
3:00	practice the trombone
4:00	read the next history chapter
5:00	memorize my lines for the school play

What was she doing at 2:00?

1. She was studying for her science test.

What had she already done?

2. She had already written an English composition.

What hadn't she done yet?

3. She hadn't practiced the trombone yet.

4. ______________________________

5. ______________________________

Brian had a very busy day at the office yesterday.

9:00	send an e-mail to the boss
10:00	give the employees their paychecks
11:00	hook up the new printer
1:00	write to the Bentley Company
2:00	take two packages to the post office

What was he doing at 11:00?

6. ______________________________

What had he already done?

7. ______________________________

8. ______________________________

What hadn't he done yet?

9. ______________________________

10. ______________________________

Mr. and Mrs. Mendoza had a very busy day at home yesterday.

8:00	assemble Billy's new bicycle
9:00	fix the fence
11:00	clean the garage
2:00	repair the roof
4:00	start to build a tree house

What were they doing at 11:00?

11. ______________________________

What had they already done?

12. ______________________________

13. ______________________________

What hadn't they done yet?

14. ______________________________

15. ______________________________

Brenda wants to lose some weight, so she had a very busy day at her health club.

9:00	do yoga
10:00	go jogging
12:00	play squash
3:00	lift weights
4:00	swim across the pool 10 times

What was she doing at 12:00?

16. ______________________________

What had she already done?

17. ______________________________

18. ______________________________

What hadn't she done yet?

19. ______________________________

20. ______________________________

F WHAT HAD THEY BEEN DOING?

1. Professor Smith finally ended his lecture at 6:00. He *(talk)* ___had been talking___ for three hours.

2. The Millers moved out of their apartment building last week. They *(live)* ________________ there for several years.

3. Our daughter lost her job last week. She *(work)* ________________ at the same company since she graduated from college.

4. Peter was happy when he and his girlfriend finally got married. They *(go out)* ________________ for eight years.

5. We were sad when Rudy's Restaurant closed. We *(plan)* ________________ to eat there on our anniversary.

6. We felt very nostalgic when we went back to our hometown. We *(think about)* ________________ going back there for a long time.

7. My husband and I were happy when our son decided to study harder. He *(get)* ________________ poor grades in school.

8. Mr. Best was happy when his neighbor bought his own ladder. He *(borrow)* ________________ Mr. Best's ladder for many years.

9. I'm not surprised that Lenny's doctor put him on a diet. Lenny *(eat)* ________________ too many fatty foods.

10. It's too bad your daughter wasn't able to perform in her violin recital last weekend. She *(rehearse)* ________________ for it for a long time.

11. I'm sorry you had to cancel your trip to Hawaii. You and your wife *(look forward)* ________________ to it for a long time.

12. I'm so happy that Sally won the marathon last weekend. She *(train)* ________________ for it for the past six months.

13. Nobody at the office was surprised when Mrs. Anderson fired Frank, her new assistant. He *(arrive)* ________________ late for work every day for the past month.

G GrammarRap: *George Had Been Thinking of Studying Greek*

Listen. Then clap and practice.

George had been thinking of studying Greek,
Moving to Athens and learning to speak.
But he changed his mind and decided to stay
With his family and friends and his dog in L.A.

Jill had been planning to learn how to ski,
But she tripped and fell and sprained her knee.
She had been dreaming of mountains and snow.
But now she's at home and has no place to go.

Marie had been planning to marry Tim,
But she fell in love with his brother, Jim.
Jim had been thinking of marrying Dee,
But everything changed when he met Marie.

H LISTENING

Listen to each word and then say it.

1. retire
2. memorize
3. practice
4. drug store
5. favorite
6. interrupt
7. around
8. restaurant
9. lively
10. loudly
11. swollen
12. elevator
13. fly
14. believe
15. cold
16. fall asleep

I MARYLOU'S BROKEN KEYBOARD

Marylou's keyboard is broken. The r's and the l's don't always work. Fill in the missing r's and l's, and then read Marylou's letters aloud.

1.

Roger,

I'm afraid the__e's something w__ong with the fi__ep__ace in the __iving __oom. A__so, the __ef__ige__ato__ is b__oken. I've been ca__ __ing the __and__o__d fo__ th__ee days on his ce__ __ phone, but he hasn't ca__ __ed back. I hope he ca__ __s me tomo__ __ow.

Ma__y__ou

2.

__ouise,

I'm te__ __ib__y wo__ __ied about my b__othe__ La__ __y's hea__th. He hu__t his __eg whi__e he was p__aying baseba__ __. He had a__ __eady dis__ocated his shou__der whi__e he was su__fing __ast F__iday. Acco__ding to his docto__, he is a__so having p__ob__ems with his b__ood p__essu__e and with his __ight w__ist. He __ea__ __y should t__y to __e__ax and take __ife a __itt__e easie__.

Ma__y__ou

3.

A__no__d,

Can you possib__y __ecommend a good __estau__ant in you__ neighbo__hood? I'm p__anning on taking my re__atives to __unch tomo__ __ow, but I'm not su__e whe__e.

We ate at a ve__y nice G__eek __estau__ant nea__ you__ apa__tment bui__ding __ast month, but I haven't been ab__e to __emembe__ the name. Do you know the p__ace?

You__ f__iend,

Ma__y__ou

4.

__osa,

I have been p__anning a t__ip to F__o__ida. I'__ __ be f__ying to O__ __ando on F__iday, and I'__ __ be __etu__ning th__ee days __ater. Have you eve__ been the__e? I __emembe__ you had fami__y membe__s who __ived in F__o__ida seve__a__ yea__s ago.

P__ease w__ite back.

A__ __ my __ove,

Ma__y__ou

J LISTENING

Listen and choose the correct answer.

1. a. He can't find it anywhere.
   b. Where can it be?
   (c.) Nobody can hear him.

2. a. No, she isn't. She's my wife.
   b. Yes. She's my wife's cousin.
   c. No. She works for a different company.

3. a. Did you take a lot of photographs?
   b. Why did you charge it?
   c. That's too bad. You had been looking forward to it.

4. a. I know. He missed all his tests.
   b. I know. He's been doing very poorly.
   c. I know. He hasn't had a bad grade yet.

5. a. Did she find it?
   b. Whose is it?
   c. I'm sure it hurt a lot.

6. a. We stayed for the lecture.
   b. We talked about classical music.
   c. We read about psychology.

7. a. Did you enjoy yourselves?
   b. How many miles did you travel?
   c. Where did you drive?

8. a. She's having problems with her feet.
   b. She's having problems with her teeth.
   c. That's okay. We all make mistakes.

9. a. Did he make it?
   b. When did you get home?
   c. I know. He likes everything you serve.

10. a. You're right. I bought one.
    b. No, but I heard the noise.
    c. Sorry. We don't sell motorcycles.

11. a. I think so. He's been working hard.
    b. Yes. His plane will leave soon.
    c. I hope so. He never goes to work.

12. a. Poor Amy! She's always sick.
    b. Amy needs a new pair of boots.
    c. She was afraid to ask for it.

13. a. What a shame! Now she can't sing.
    b. What a shame! Now she can't knit.
    c. What a shame! Now she can't walk.

14. a. Would you like to talk about it?
    b. Who are you going to give it to?
    c. What did you decide to do?

15. a. I like you, too.
    b. What are you going to send me?
    c. You don't have anything to be jealous about.

16. a. Was it a very bad accident?
    b. Do you know anybody who can fix it?
    c. How long had they been going out?

17. a. I hope he feels better soon.
    b. What happened? Did you twist it?
    c. How are your cousins?

18. a. Did you call the doctor?
    b. What had you eaten?
    c. Why were you sad?

19. a. I'm glad to hear that.
    b. What was he angry about?
    c. What did he ask them?

20. a. We enjoyed the music.
    b. The lecture was very boring.
    c. The food was excellent.

21. a. They're too small.
    b. You have a job interview today.
    c. You have a baseball game today.

22. a. She enjoys going to the symphony.
    b. She enjoys going window-shopping.
    c. She enjoys doing gymnastics.

23. a. We're going to have a party.
    b. We're going on vacation.
    c. We received a lot of anniversary gifts.

24. a. He's glad he bought it.
    b. He's going to wear it for several years.
    c. He has to return it on Tuesday.

✓ CHECK-UP TEST: Chapters 7–8

A. Complete the sentences with the appropriate verb form.

(eat) **1.** Why do you keep on ______________ junk food?

(wrestle) **2.** My mother thinks ________________ is dangerous.

(stop) **3.** I've decided ________________ interrupting people all the time.

(box) **4.** Bruno practices ______________ every day at the gym.

(swim) **5.** ________________ is a good way to relax.

(skate) **6.** Where did your daughter learn __________________ so well?

(talk) **7.** Please stop __________________. I'm trying to sleep!

(do) **8.** Rita thinks that ____________ exercises is a good way to start the day.

B. Complete the sentences, using the past perfect tense.

Ex. *(wear)* I wore my favorite striped tie to work yesterday. I __hadn't worn__ it to work in a long time.

(start) By the time Andrew got to the play, it __had__ already __started__.

(speak) **1.** I had dinner with some Japanese friends last night. I enjoyed myself very much because I ____________________ Japanese in a long time.

(do) **2.** By the time Jennifer's father got home from work, she ________ already ____________ her homework, and she was ready to play baseball in the yard with him.

(leave) **3.** Ronald was upset. By the time he got to the train, it ________ already __________.

(write) **4.** I wrote an e-mail to my grandparents last night because I ____________________ to them for a few weeks.

(have) **5.** Patty had pizza for lunch yesterday. She ______________________ pizza in a long time.

(take) **6.** My husband and I took a walk after dinner last night. We ____________________ a walk after dinner in a long time.

(eat) **7.** I ate a big piece of chocolate cake last night and felt terrible about it. I _________ ____________________ a rich dessert since I started my diet.

(go) **8.** My parents went back to their hometown last month. They __________________ back there for twenty years.

C. Complete the sentences, using the past perfect continuous tense.

Ex. *(study)* Jonathan was glad he did well on his astronomy exam. He <u>had been studying</u> for it for days.

(work) **1.** Marvin didn't get his promotion at work. He was heartbroken because he ______________________ overtime for several months.

(train) **2.** I was disappointed they canceled the marathon last week. I ______________ ______________ for it since last summer.

(argue) **3.** Jane and John broke up last night. They ______________________ with each other for the past several weeks.

(plan) **4.** Nancy caught a cold and couldn't go on her camping trip. It's a shame because she ______________________ it since last April.

D. Listen and choose the correct answer.

Ex. (a.) go fishing.
b. going canoeing.

1. a. tease her little brother.
b. interrupting people.

2. a. moving to Miami.
b. to sell our house.

3. a. to buy a sports car.
b. buying a sports car.

4. a. waiting in line.
b. drive downtown.

5. a. going out with Richard.
b. ask for a raise.

A WHAT ARE THEY SAYING?

1. A. Did you pick up Rover at the vet?

B. No. I didn't ___pick him up___.
I thought YOU did.

2. A. Did you turn on the heat?

B. Yes. I ______________ a few hours ago, but it's still cold in here.

3. A. You should take back these library books.

B. I know. I'll ______________ tomorrow morning.

4. A. Has Diane filled out her income tax forms?

B. No. She's going to ______________ this weekend.

5. A. Where should we hang up this portrait?

B. Let's ______________ over the fireplace.

6. A. I'm having trouble hooking up my computer.

B. No problem. I'll ______________.

7. A. Are you ever going to throw out these old souvenirs?

B. I'll ______________ some day.

8. A. Did Sally take back her cell phone to the store?

B. Yes. She ______________ this afternoon.

9. A. Did your daughter take down the photographs of her old boyfriend?

B. Yes. She ______________ as soon as they stopped going out.

10. A. Did you remember to call up Aunt Clara to wish her "Happy Birthday"?

B. Sorry. I didn't ______________.
I forgot it was her birthday.

B WHAT ARE THEY SAYING?

bring back	hand in	put away	put on	take off	turn off	turn on	wake up

1. I think we should ___turn on___ the air conditioner. It's getting very hot in here.
   Good idea. I'll ______________ right away.

2. When are you going to ___hand___ your biology report ___in___?
   I'm going to ______________ tomorrow morning. I have to write it tonight.

3. Let's ______________ Mom and Dad! It's 8:00, and they're still sleeping!
   Don't ______________. It's Saturday. They don't go to work today.

4. Don't forget to ______________ the printer __________ before you leave the office tonight.
   You don't have to worry. I always ______________ before I leave.

5. Why don't you ______________ your hat and coat? It's warm in here.
   I'll ______________ in a few minutes. I'm still a little cold.

6. Susie, when are you going to __________ your toys __________?
   I'm still playing with them. I'll ______________ later.

7. Teddy, it's time for bed. __________ your pajamas __________!
   Okay, Dad. I'll ______________ in a few minutes.

8. Do you think Richard will __________ his girlfriend __________ to the house after the dance?
   I don't know. Maybe he'll ______________. I hope he does. I really want to meet her.

C GrammarRap: *I Don't Know How!*

Listen. Then clap and practice.

A. Take off your skis.
Take them off now!
B. I can't take them off.
I don't know how!

A. Turn off the engine!
Turn it off now!
B. I can't turn it off.
I don't know how!

A. Turn on the oven!
Turn it on now!
B. I can't turn it on.
I don't know how!

A. Hook up the printer!
Hook it up now!
B. I can't hook it up.
I don't know how!

A. Pick up the suitcase.
Give it to Jack.
B. I can't pick it up.
I have a bad back!

A. Take back the videos!
Take them back today.
B. I can't take them back.
It's a holiday!

D WHAT ARE THEY SAYING?

cross out	give back	look up	throw away	turn off
do over	hook up	think over	turn down	write down

1.

2. A. Do we still have the hammer we borrowed from our next-door neighbors?

   B. No, we don't. We ____________________ a long time ago.

3. A. What's the matter with the answering machine? Is it broken?

   B. No, it isn't. I forgot to ______________________________.

4. A. Are you going to accept the invitation to Roger's wedding?

   B. I don't know. I have to ____________________ carefully. His wedding is in Alaska.

5. A. What's the weather forecast for tomorrow?

   B. I'm not sure. You should ________________________ on the Internet.

6. A. Is Kimberly going to the prom with Frank?

   B. No, she isn't. She had to ________________________ because she already had a date with somebody else.

7. A. What should I do with all these letters from my ex-boyfriend?

   B. I think you should ______________________________.

8. A. What's Walter's new address?

   B. I can't remember. But I know I've ____________________ somewhere.

9. A. Should I erase all these mistakes in my math homework?

   B. No, I think you should just ____________________________.

10.

E WHAT'S THE WORD?

James just moved into a new apartment. What does he have to do?

1. He has to (put away / throw away) his books and his clothes. [put away circled]
2. He has to (fill out / hook up) his printer and his computer.
3. He has to (take out / take back) the moving truck he rented.

Jennifer is very happy and excited. She just got engaged. What's she going to do?

4. She's going to (wake up / drop off) her parents and tell them the news.
5. She's going to (call off / call up) all her friends.
6. She's going to (look up / write down) all the things her boyfriend said.

Mr. and Mrs. Baker's aunt and uncle are going to visit them next week. What do the Bakers have to do before then?

7. They have to (clean up / take out) their apartment.
8. They have to (pick out / put away) their children's toys.
9. They have to (throw out / hook up) all their old newspapers.
10. They have to (call up / hang up) their aunt and uncle's portrait.

F WHAT SHOULD THEY DO?

figure out	look up	throw out	use up
give back	think over	turn off	wake up

1. 

2. A. I've been using my neighbor's screwdriver all summer.
   B. Don't you think it's time to _______________?
3. A. Is there any more sugar?
   B. No. We _______________. We have to buy some tomorrow.
4. A. I don't know the definition of this word.
   B. You really should _______________ in the dictionary.
5. A. This math problem is very difficult.
   B. Maybe your mother can help you _______________.
6. A. It's 7:30, and the children are still sleeping.
   B. They're going to be late for school. I'll _______________.
7. A. It's really cold in here! Is the air conditioner on?
   B. Yes, it is. I'll _______________ right away.
8. A. I'm very embarrassed. These are the worst photographs anyone has ever taken of me.
   B. Well, if they bother you that much, why don't you _______________?

G LISTENING

Listen and choose the correct answer.

1. a. picked it up.
   (b.) used it up.
2. a. turn it down.
   b. turn it on.
3. a. take them down.
   b. turn them down.
4. a. think them over.
   b. drop them off.
5. a. hook it up.
   b. look it up.
6. a. give it back?
   b. hand it in?
7. a. throw it out.
   b. figure it out.
8. a. write it down.
   b. use it up.
9. a. pick it up.
   b. clean it up.

H COME UP WITH THE RIGHT ANSWER

call on	get over	look through	pick on	take after
get along with	hear from	look up to	run into	

1. 
I ___take after___ my father. We're both athletic, we're both interested in engineering, and we both like to paint. I'm really glad I ___take after him___.

2. 
I haven't ______________ my son in three weeks. He's at college, and I usually ______________ every week!

3. 
I'm so embarrassed. My teacher ______________ me twice in class today, but I didn't know ANY of the answers. I have to study tonight. She might ______________ again tomorrow.

4. 
My husband and I enjoyed ______________ our wedding pictures. We hadn't ______________ in years.

5. 
Jack ______________ his cold very quickly. I think he ______________ fast because he stayed home and took care of himself.

6. 
I really ______________ my grandmother. She's honest, she's intelligent, and she's very generous. I hope someday when I'm a grandmother, my grandchildren will ______________, too.

7. 
I was very surprised. I ______________ my old girlfriend at the bank yesterday morning. And then I ______________ again at a movie last night.

8. 
I don't ______________ my mother-in-law. We often disagree. All the people in our family ______________. Why can't I?

9. 
Bobby is mean. He ______________ his cats all the time. The cats don't like it when Bobby ______________.

I GrammarRap: *I Don't Get Along with Kate and Clem*

Listen. Then clap and practice.

I don't get along with Kate and Clem.
I almost never hear from them.
But I get along well with Bob and Fay.
I call them up three times a day.

Jack takes after his Uncle Jim.
Bob looks up to his father, Tim.
Kate never picks on her sister, Sue.
But she always picks on her brother, Lou.

J CHOOSE

1. A. Do we have any more pens?
   B. No, we don't. We ______.
   a. ran into them
   (b.) ran out of them
2. A. Does Carol still have the flu?
   B. No. She ______ a few days ago.
   a. got over it
   b. got it over
3. A. Does Jill get along with her brother?
   B. No. He ______ all the time.
   a. picks her on
   b. picks on her
4. A. I can't remember Tom's phone number.
   B. You should ______.
   a. look up to him
   b. look it up
5. A. Amy knows all the answers in class.
   B. Does the teacher always ______?
   a. call on her
   b. call her on
6. A. This is a very difficult problem.
   B. I know. I can't ______.
   a. figure out it
   b. figure it out
7. A. Have you heard from Pam recently?
   B. Yes. I ______ the other day.
   a. heard her from
   b. heard from her
8. A. What should I do with these old letters?
   B. Why don't you ______?
   a. throw them out
   b. throw out them
9. A. These photographs are wonderful!
   B. I know. Let's ______ again.
   a. look through them
   b. look them through
10. A. Do you like William?
    B. Oh, yes. I ______ very well.
    a. get him along
    b. get along with him
11. A. Should I turn off the computer?
    B. No. You can ______.
    a. leave it on
    b. leave on it
12. A. Did you hang up your uncle's portrait?
    B. No, I didn't. I ______.
    a. took it down
    b. took down it
13. A. You look like your father.
    B. I know. Everybody says I ______.
    a. take him after
    b. take after him
14. A. They have a very unusual last name.
    B. You'll remember it if you ______.
    a. write down it
    b. write it down

K WHAT DOES IT MEAN?

Choose the correct answer.

1. Richard takes after his mother.
   a. He's always with her.
   (b.) They're both shy.
   c. His mother always arrives first.

2. Please turn off the air conditioner.
   a. It's too hot in this room.
   b. The room is too small.
   c. It's too cold in this room.

3. Tom left his briefcase on the plane.
   a. Maybe his mind slipped.
   b. He forgot it.
   c. He was very careful.

4. I'm going to take these pants back.
   a. They're new.
   b. They're medium.
   c. They're too baggy.

5. Fran can't find her notebook.
   a. I hope she didn't throw it out.
   b. I hope she didn't fill it out.
   c. I hope she didn't take it off.

6. Bob doesn't get along with his neighbors.
   a. He can't stand to talk to them.
   b. He likes them very much.
   c. He looks up to them.

7. I hope I don't run into my old boyfriend.
   a. Why? Will he get hurt?
   b. Why don't you want to see him?
   c. Why? Does he like to jog?

8. Paul had to do his homework over.
   a. It was excellent.
   b. He didn't think it over.
   c. He had made a lot of mistakes.

L LISTENING

Listen and choose the correct answer.

1. a. He's very tall.
   b. I can never find him.
   (c.) I want to be like him.

2. a. You're lucky he has a car.
   b. I'm sure that bothers you.
   c. Do you also pick him up?

3. a. Yes. I put it in the closet.
   b. Yes. I gave it to our neighbor.
   c. Yes. We had used it all up.

4. a. I'm sorry you're still sick.
   b. I'm glad you're feeling better.
   c. It's too bad you have to do it over.

5. a. No. He speaks very softly.
   b. Yes. He sent me an e-mail yesterday.
   c. No. I haven't heard him recently.

6. a. The music was very loud.
   b. Somebody had picked it up.
   c. I already had another date.

7. a. Yes, several times.
   b. Yes, but I wasn't home.
   c. Yes, but I had already left the house.

8. a. He didn't need it anymore.
   b. It was already at the cleaner's.
   c. I know. He found one he really liked.

9. a. Did she hurt herself?
   b. How did you hurt yourself?
   c. When does her plane leave?

10. a. The store isn't having a sale.
    b. Everything in the store is cheaper.
    c. Everything is 20 cents less this week.

11. a. Good. I'll buy it.
    b. Don't worry. We have larger ones.
    c. I know. It's too tight.

12. a. Yes. I used up four pair.
    b. Yes. I put on four pair.
    c. Yes. I looked up four pair.

A NOT THE ONLY ONE

10

1.

2.

3.

4.

5.

6.

7.

8.

9.

10.

11.

B WHAT A COINCIDENCE!

A. Do you live near here?

B. Yes. I live on Center Street.

A. Really? So __do I__ [1]. I live in the new apartment building at the corner of Center Street and Broadway.

B. What a coincidence! ____________ [2], too. I guess we're neighbors. My name is Frank Winters.

A. Hi. I'm Steve Green. Nice to meet you.

B. Nice meeting you, too. So how long have you been living there?

A. I moved in last week.

B. What a coincidence! ____________ [3], too. I've been very busy since I got here.

A. So ____________ [4]. Moving into a new apartment isn't easy.

B. You're right. It isn't. Tell me, have you found a job yet?

A. Yes, I have. I'll be working at Mason's Department Store.

B. I don't believe it! ____________ [5], too.

A. What department will you be working in?

B. I got a job in the Men's Clothing Department.

A. What a coincidence! So ____________ [6]. I was a salesperson in my last job also.

B. ____________ [7], too. I sold men's clothing.

A. I can't believe it! ____________ [8], too.

B. I'm on my way to work right now.

A. ____________ [9], too. Do you want to have lunch together?

B. Sure. I have a lunch break at noon.

A. So ____________ [10]. Let's meet for lunch in the company cafeteria.

B. Okay. That'll be nice. I'm looking forward to it.

A. So ____________ [11].

C NOT THE ONLY ONE

1.

2.

3.

4.

5.

6.

7.

8.

9.

10.

11.

D LISTENING

Listen and complete the sentences.

1. So did I.
2. ______________, too.
3. So ______________.
4. ______________ either.
5. ______________, too.
6. ______________, too.
7. Neither ______________.
8. ______________, too.
9. Neither ______________.
10. So ______________.
11. ______________ either.
12. ______________, too.
13. Neither ______________.
14. So ______________.
15. ______________ either.

E GRAMMARRAP: *So Do I*

Listen. Then clap and practice.

A. I like to fly.
B. So do I.
A. They like to ski.
B. So do we.
A. She likes the zoo.
B. He does, too.
A. You're a good friend.
B. So are you.

F GRAMMARRAP: *They Didn't Either*

Listen. Then clap and practice.

We didn't eat it.
They didn't either.
He didn't finish it.
Neither did she.
She wasn't hungry.
He wasn't either.
They weren't hungry.
Neither were we.

G WHAT ARE THEY SAYING?

1. Why were you and your brother late for school today?
   I had to go to the dentist, and so ___did he___.

2. Will you and your wife be home this evening?
   I don't think so. I'll be working late, and so ______________.

3. How did you and Tom feel after you ran in the marathon?
   I was exhausted, and ______________, too.

4. Would you and your sister like to learn how to ski?
   Actually, I've already tried it, and so ______________.

5. Can Ricky and I go to the movies tonight?
   He should study for his English exam, and ______________, too.

6. Have you seen Mr. and Mrs. Martinez recently?
   I saw them today. I was in the park, and ______________, too.

7. Should I go into the water with Timmy and Susie?
   No. That's okay. Timmy can swim, and ______________ Susie.

8. Why weren't you and your brother at baseball practice today?
   I had to help my mother, and so ______________.

9. Why are you and your wife leaving the party?
   She has to get up early tomorrow, and ______________, too.

10. Why are your parents so worried?
   I've decided to ....
   ....,
   and ____________ my brother.

H WHAT ARE THEY SAYING?

1. 
Are you and your brother going to be in the school play?
Unfortunately, he can't act, and neither ___can I___.

2. 
Why do you and your friends look so upset?
I didn't do very well on the math test, and ______________ either.

3. 
Did you and your son see the baseball game on TV today?
No, we didn't. I'm not interested in sports, and neither ______________.

4. 
Are you and your sister going to go to the concert tonight?
No, we aren't. I don't like folk music, and ______________ either.

5. 
Why did you and your friends leave the dance so early last night?
I wasn't having a very good time, and neither ______________.

6. 
Have you and your wife made plans for your vacation yet?
I haven't had very much time, and ______________ either.

7. 
Are you and your roommates going to Sally's wedding?
No, we aren't. I won't be here this weekend, and neither ______________.

8. 
It's getting late. Should I make dinner now?
The truth is, I'm not very hungry, and the children ______________.

9. 
Is the DVD player still broken?
Yes, it is. I haven't been able to fix it, and ______________ your father.

10. 
How was your date with Samantha last night?
We were both a little nervous. I had never gone out on a date before, and ______________ either.

I WHAT ARE THEY SAYING?

so	too	either	neither

1. A. Why didn't Ronald and his wife go to work yesterday?

   B. He had a terrible cold,

   and { so did she.
   { she did, too.

2. A. Did Betty and Bob enjoy the concert last night?

   B. Not really. She couldn't hear the music,

   and { ______________.
   { ______________.

3. A. Do Jack and his girlfriend enjoy going sailing?

   B. No, they don't. She gets seasick,

   and { ______________.
   { ______________.

4. A. Why didn't Mr. and Mrs. Miller order the cheesecake for dessert?

   B. He doesn't eat rich foods,

   and { ______________.
   { ______________.

5. A. Why did Beverly and Brian have trouble doing their chemistry experiments?

   B. He hadn't followed the instructions,

   and { ______________.
   { ______________.

6. A. Why aren't you and Peter good friends any more?

   B. I'm in love with Amanda Richardson,

   and { ______________.
   { ______________.

J OUR FAMILY

1. I'm tall, but my sister and brother ___aren't___. I've always __________ the tallest person in our family.

2. My brother isn't very athletic, but my sister __________. She enjoys __________ squash and __________ gymnastics.

3. I can't draw pictures, but my brother __________. He's been __________ pictures since he __________ four years old.

4. My brother and I have different interests. I enjoy seeing movies, but my brother __________. He enjoys __________ to lectures and concerts.

5. My mother is interested in photography, but my father __________. My mother __________ photographs since she was a teenager.

6. My father has lived here all his life, but his parents __________. They've __________ in this country __________ fifty years. Before that, they __________ in Italy.

7. My grandparents sometimes speak to us in Italian, but my father __________. He __________ Italian to anyone in a long time.

8. I'll be going to college next year, but my brother __________. He __________ finished high school yet.

9. I don't have a very good voice, but my sister __________. She sings in the school choir. She has __________ in the choir __________ she started high school.

10. I'm usually very neat, but my sister and brother __________. They never hang __________ their clothes or put __________ their books.

11. I know how to ski, but my brother __________. I've been skiing __________ the past nine years.

12. My sister is a very good skater, but my brother and I __________. We just started __________ a month ago. Before that, we __________ never __________ at all.

K LISTENING

Listen and complete the sentences.

1. but my husband ______didn't______.
2. but my daughter ____________________.
3. but you ____________________.
4. but I ____________________.
5. but my friends ____________________.
6. but my wife ____________________.
7. but you ____________________.
8. but my brother ____________________.
9. but everybody else ____________________.
10. but our teacher ____________________.
11. but my son ____________________.
12. but the other man ____________________.
13. but my sister ____________________.
14. but I ____________________.
15. but my friends ____________________.
16. but my brother ____________________.
17. but my children ____________________.
18. but I ____________________.

L GRAMMARRAP: *I've Been Working Hard, and You Have, Too*

Listen. Then clap and practice.

I've been working hard, and		you have,	too.
I'm	exhausted,	and so	are you.
He's been	out of town,	and so	has she.
They've been very	busy,	and so	have we.
I	didn't go,	and neither	did he.
They	weren't there,	and neither	were we.
We	stayed home,	and so	did they.
Nobody	went	to the meeting	that day.
I don't speak	Greek,	but my brother	does.
I wasn't born in	Greece,	but my mother	was.
I didn't study	Greek,	but my brother	did.
He's spoken	Greek	since he was	a kid.

M SOUND IT OUT!

Listen to each word and then say it.

full		fool	
1. look	3. put	1. noon	3. Judy
2. could	4. foot	2. drew	4. food

Listen and put a circle around the word that has the same sound.

1. full:	pool	cooks	shoe
2. flu:	too	would	blood
3. good:	soup	shouldn't	June
4. wood:	flu	tooth	put
5. could:	cup	cookies	upstairs
6. hook:	food	movie	good
7. woman:	sugar	true	new

Now make a sentence using all the words you circled, and read the sentence aloud.

8. ________ ________ ________ ________ ________ much ________ in their ________.

9. suit:	two	put	bus
10. cook:	food	books	sunny
11. foot:	bookcase	pool	must
12. blue:	just	who	looked
13. would:	suit	tool	took
14. cool:	stood	afternoon	pulse
15. school:	Susan's	thunder	floor

Now make a sentence using all the words you circled, and read the sentence aloud.

16. ________ ________ ________ ________ from ________ ________ this ________?

N WHAT DOES IT MEAN?

j	1. afford	a.	afraid
______	2. argue	b.	do poorly
______	3. bachelor	c.	fight
______	4. begin	d.	finish
______	5. bump into	e.	friendly and talkative
______	6. can't stand	f.	give back
______	7. compatible	g.	give lessons
______	8. consider	h.	hate
______	9. continue	i.	have a lot in common
______	10. discuss	j.	have enough money
______	11. exam	k.	how much it costs
______	12. exhausted	l.	hurt
______	13. fail	m.	keep on
______	14. frightened	n.	meet
______	15. hike	o.	ready
______	16. injure	p.	recently
______	17. lately	q.	single man
______	18. outgoing	r.	someone who doesn't eat meat
______	19. prepared	s.	start
______	20. price	t.	study again
______	21. return	u.	take a long walk
______	22. review	v.	talk about
______	23. stand in line	w.	test
______	24. teach	x.	think about
______	25. use up	y.	tired
______	26. vegetarian	z.	wait

✓ CHECK-UP TEST: Chapters 9-10

A. Complete the sentences.

Ex. My son is waiting for me at the bus stop. I have to pick ___him___ ___up___ right away.

My mother and I are both tall with curly hair. Everybody says I take ___after___ ___her___.

1. I'll finish my homework in a little while, and then I'll hand __________ __________.
2. My father is a very smart man. I really look __________ __________ __________.
3. I haven't talked to Aunt Shirley lately. I hope I hear __________ __________ soon.
4. My English teacher didn't like my composition. I have to do __________ __________.
5. I don't know the definition of this word. I need to look __________ __________.
6. I can't find any flour. I think we ran __________ __________ __________.
7. I can't find my wallet. Could you help me look __________ __________?
8. Don't leave your clothes on the bed. You really should hang __________ __________.
9. Don't worry about your mistakes. You can always cross __________ __________.
10. I can never remember Alan's address. I should write __________ __________.
11. I've had the flu for the past several days. My doctor says I'll get __________ __________ soon.

B. Complete the sentences.

so	too	neither	either

Ex. Maria did well on her science test, and ___so did___ her sister.

1. I'm wearing new shoes today, and ______________ my brother.
2. I won't be able to come to the meeting tomorrow, and ______________ Barbara.
3. I was bored during Professor Gray's lecture, and my friends ______________.
4. Janet can't skate, and her brother ______________.
5. I've been taking guitar lessons for years, and ______________ my sisters.
6. David worked overtime yesterday, and his wife ______________.
7. Louise has never been to Europe, and ______________ her husband.
8. I want to complain to the landlord, and ______________ my neighbors.
9. I'm not very athletic, and ______________ my wife.

C. Listen and complete the sentences.

Ex. but her husband ___doesn't___.

1. but my sister ______________.
2. but my parents ______________.
3. but my brother ______________.
4. but my wife ______________.
5. but I ______________.

ACHIEVEMENT TESTS

Name ______________________

Date ______________ Class ______________

1

A PERSONAL INFORMATION FORM

Name: (1) ______________________

Address: (2) ______________________

City: (3) ______________ State: (4) ______ Zip Code: (5) ______

Social Security Number: (6) ______________ Country of Origin: (7) ______

Telephone: (8) ______ E-mail: (9) ______ Date of Birth: (10) ______

Height: (11) ______ Eye Color: (12) ______ Hair Color: (13) ______ Marital Status: (14) ______

Family Members in Household (Name—Relationship):

(15) ______________ ______________

Look at the information. Choose the correct line on the form.

1. 11/14/88
- Ⓐ Line 5
- Ⓑ Line 6
- Ⓒ Line 8
- Ⓓ Line 10

2. 224-67-8139
- Ⓐ Line 5
- Ⓑ Line 6
- Ⓒ Line 8
- Ⓓ Line 10

3. Mexico
- Ⓐ Line 3
- Ⓑ Line 4
- Ⓒ Line 7
- Ⓓ Line 10

4. 1263 Main St.
- Ⓐ Line 2
- Ⓑ Line 7
- Ⓒ Line 9
- Ⓓ Line 15

5. 5'9"
- Ⓐ Line 5
- Ⓑ Line 6
- Ⓒ Line 10
- Ⓓ Line 11

6. married
- Ⓐ Line 7
- Ⓑ Line 12
- Ⓒ Line 14
- Ⓓ Line 15

7. FL
- Ⓐ Line 3
- Ⓑ Line 4
- Ⓒ Line 5
- Ⓓ Line 14

8. blue
- Ⓐ Line 11
- Ⓑ Line 12
- Ⓒ Line 13
- Ⓓ Line 14

9. (305) 965-4213
- Ⓐ Line 5
- Ⓑ Line 6
- Ⓒ Line 8
- Ⓓ Line 9

10. Alma Suarez—wife
- Ⓐ Line 1
- Ⓑ Line 2
- Ⓒ Line 14
- Ⓓ Line 15

11. Miami
- Ⓐ Line 3
- Ⓑ Line 4
- Ⓒ Line 5
- Ⓓ Line 9

12. cjs24@msl.com
- Ⓐ Line 2
- Ⓑ Line 3
- Ⓒ Line 8
- Ⓓ Line 9

1 Ⓐ Ⓑ Ⓒ Ⓓ	4 Ⓐ Ⓑ Ⓒ Ⓓ	7 Ⓐ Ⓑ Ⓒ Ⓓ	10 Ⓐ Ⓑ Ⓒ Ⓓ
2 Ⓐ Ⓑ Ⓒ Ⓓ	5 Ⓐ Ⓑ Ⓒ Ⓓ	8 Ⓐ Ⓑ Ⓒ Ⓓ	11 Ⓐ Ⓑ Ⓒ Ⓓ
3 Ⓐ Ⓑ Ⓒ Ⓓ	6 Ⓐ Ⓑ Ⓒ Ⓓ	9 Ⓐ Ⓑ Ⓒ Ⓓ	12 Ⓐ Ⓑ Ⓒ Ⓓ

Go to the next page

B GRAMMAR IN CONTEXT: Small Talk at Work

Choose the correct answer to complete the conversations.

13. What are you _____?

- (A) reading
- (B) looking
- (C) read
- (D) look

14. _____ a book about the president.

- (A) I read
- (B) I'm reading
- (C) I watch
- (D) I'm watching

15. Do you _____ biographies?

- (A) reading
- (B) like to
- (C) like to read
- (D) liking

16. Yes. _____ them whenever I can.

- (A) I read
- (B) I'm reading
- (C) I like
- (D) I like to

17. _____ swim?

- (A) You like
- (B) You like to
- (C) You do like to
- (D) Do you like to

18. No. _____ a very good swimmer.

- (A) I don't
- (B) I'm not
- (C) You're
- (D) You aren't

19. _____ exercise?

- (A) You often
- (B) How often you
- (C) How often do you
- (D) Do you how often

20. I exercise _____.

- (A) three times
- (B) three times a week
- (C) three weeks
- (D) every

21. What do you like to do _____?

- (A) in your free time
- (B) in your time
- (C) in your free
- (D) when your free time

22. I like to _____.

- (A) tennis player
- (B) tennis
- (C) playing tennis
- (D) play tennis

13 (A) (B) (C) (D)	16 (A) (B) (C) (D)	19 (A) (B) (C) (D)	21 (A) (B) (C) (D)
14 (A) (B) (C) (D)	17 (A) (B) (C) (D)	20 (A) (B) (C) (D)	22 (A) (B) (C) (D)
15 (A) (B) (C) (D)	18 (A) (B) (C) (D)		

Go to the next page

Name ______________________ Date ____________

C CLOZE READING: Grading Systems

Choose the correct answers to complete the paragraph.

There (A) am (B) is (C) are [filled] different types of grading systems (A) out (B) in (C) between [23] different schools. Some schools (A) use (B) uses (C) using [24] a letter marking system with the letters A, B, C, D, (A) between (B) and (C) for [25] F. (A) Other (B) Others (C) Another [26] schools use the letters E, G, F, and P to describe students as Excellent, (A) Grade (B) Get (C) Good [27], Fair, or (A) Pretty (B) Popular (C) Poor [28]. Some schools (A) don't (B) doesn't (C) aren't [29] use letter grades. They use (A) number (B) numbers (C) names [30] such as 75%, 80%, 85% or they don't use grades at all.

D READING: The Education System

Look at the table. Choose the correct answer.

Here is a table that shows the levels of high school and college in the education system in the United States. Notice that we use the same words to describe the levels of students in both parts of the education system. Study the table. Then do Numbers 31 through 34.

HIGH SCHOOL GRADE	LEVEL	YEAR OF COLLEGE
9	Freshman	1
10	Sophomore	2
11	Junior	3
12	Senior	4

31. Carla is a junior in high school. What grade is she in?

- (A) Grade 9.
- (B) Grade 10.
- (C) Grade 11.
- (D) Grade 12.

32. Martin is in his last year as a student at Carleton College. Which sentence is correct?

- (A) He's in Grade 9.
- (B) He's a freshman.
- (C) He's in Grade 12.
- (D) He's a senior.

33. Wendy is a sophomore. She's 20 years old. Which sentence is probably true?

- (A) Wendy goes to high school.
- (B) Wendy goes to college.
- (C) Wendy is in the 10th grade.
- (D) Wendy was a junior last year.

34. The paragraph describes two parts of the education system. What is another part of the education system that isn't described in the paragraph?

- (A) Elementary schools.
- (B) High schools.
- (C) Colleges.
- (D) Supermarkets.

23 (A) (B) (C) (D)	26 (A) (B) (C) (D)	29 (A) (B) (C) (D)	32 (A) (B) (C) (D)
24 (A) (B) (C) (D)	27 (A) (B) (C) (D)	30 (A) (B) (C) (D)	33 (A) (B) (C) (D)
25 (A) (B) (C) (D)	28 (A) (B) (C) (D)	31 (A) (B) (C) (D)	34 (A) (B) (C) (D)

Go to the next page

E LISTENING ASSESSMENT: An Automated Message

Read and listen to the questions. Then listen to the automated telephone message and answer the questions.

35. How can you listen to the information in Spanish?
   - (A) Press 1.
   - (B) Press 2.
   - (C) Press 3.
   - (D) Press 4.

36. How can you listen to the information in Arabic?
   - (A) Press 4.
   - (B) Press 5.
   - (C) Press 6.
   - (D) Press 7.

37. How many days a week is the program open?
   - (A) Two.
   - (B) Three.
   - (C) Five.
   - (D) Seven.

38. When can you take a placement test for fall English classes?
   - (A) August 26.
   - (B) September 3.
   - (C) September 10.
   - (D) September 26.

39. On what date do fall classes begin?
   - (A) September 2.
   - (B) September 3.
   - (C) September 10.
   - (D) 8:30 A.M.

40. How can you listen to the information again?
   - (A) Press 1.
   - (B) Press S.
   - (C) Press #.
   - (D) Press *.

F WRITING ASSESSMENT: A Personal Information Form

Name: ______________________________

Address: ______________________________

City: ____________ State: ______ Zip Code: ________

Social Security Number: ____________ Country of Origin: ____________

Telephone: ____________ E-mail: ____________ Date of Birth: ____________

Height: ______ Eye Color: ______ Hair Color: ______ Marital Status: ______

Family Members in Household (Name—Relationship):

______________________ ______________________

______________________ ______________________

G SPEAKING ASSESSMENT

I can ask and answer these questions:

Ask	Answer	
☐	☐	Where are you from?
☐	☐	Where do you live now?
☐	☐	Are you married?
☐	☐	Are you single?
☐	☐	Who are the people in your family?
☐	☐	Do you work or go to school?
☐	☐	What do you do/study?
☐	☐	What do you like to do in your free time?

35 (A) (B) (C) (D)   37 (A) (B) (C) (D)   39 (A) (B) (C) (D)

36 (A) (B) (C) (D)   38 (A) (B) (C) (D)   40 (A) (B) (C) (D)

STOP

Name ______________________

Date ______________ Class ______________

2

A SMALL TALK ABOUT PAST EVENTS

Choose the correct answer.

Example:

My children ____ sick yesterday.
- Ⓐ are
- Ⓑ is
- Ⓒ was
- ● were

1. Traffic ____ very bad this morning.
- Ⓐ are
- Ⓑ be
- Ⓒ was
- Ⓓ were

2. I ____ a movie last night.
- Ⓐ go
- Ⓑ went
- Ⓒ see
- Ⓓ saw

3. I ____ sleep well last night.
- Ⓐ don't
- Ⓑ didn't
- Ⓒ am not
- Ⓓ doesn't

4. Did you ____ today?
- Ⓐ the bus
- Ⓑ bus to work
- Ⓒ take the bus
- Ⓓ took the bus

5. What ____ last weekend?
- Ⓐ did you do
- Ⓑ do you did
- Ⓒ you do
- Ⓓ you did

6. Our supervisor ____ very angry this morning.
- Ⓐ did
- Ⓑ was
- Ⓒ be
- Ⓓ were

7. ____ you nervous while the boss was visiting our department?
- Ⓐ Are
- Ⓑ Will
- Ⓒ Was
- Ⓓ Were

8. ____ a good vacation?
- Ⓐ You had
- Ⓑ Did you had
- Ⓒ Did you have
- Ⓓ Had you

9. I ____ an accident while I ____ to work today.
- Ⓐ see . . . was driving
- Ⓑ saw . . . was driving
- Ⓒ saw . . . am driving
- Ⓓ was seeing . . . drove

1 Ⓐ Ⓑ Ⓒ Ⓓ	4 Ⓐ Ⓑ Ⓒ Ⓓ	7 Ⓐ Ⓑ Ⓒ Ⓓ
2 Ⓐ Ⓑ Ⓒ Ⓓ	5 Ⓐ Ⓑ Ⓒ Ⓓ	8 Ⓐ Ⓑ Ⓒ Ⓓ
3 Ⓐ Ⓑ Ⓒ Ⓓ	6 Ⓐ Ⓑ Ⓒ Ⓓ	9 Ⓐ Ⓑ Ⓒ Ⓓ

Go to the next page

B GRAMMAR IN CONTEXT: Apologizing & Making Excuses

Choose the correct answer to complete the conversations.

Ex: _____ I arrived late this morning.
- Ⓐ I sorry
- ● I'm sorry
- Ⓒ You sorry
- Ⓓ You're sorry

10. What _____?
- Ⓐ happen
- Ⓑ happens
- Ⓒ happening
- Ⓓ happened

11. My car _____ while I was driving to work.
- Ⓐ broke down
- Ⓑ break down
- Ⓒ breaks down
- Ⓓ breaking down

12. _____ bad.
- Ⓐ You
- Ⓑ You're too
- Ⓒ That's too
- Ⓓ That

13. I want to _____.
- Ⓐ apology
- Ⓑ apologize
- Ⓒ apologizing
- Ⓓ sorry

14. For _____?
- Ⓐ what
- Ⓑ when
- Ⓒ why
- Ⓓ how

15. I _____ finish my work today.
- Ⓐ do
- Ⓑ did
- Ⓒ could
- Ⓓ couldn't

16. _____ not?
- Ⓐ You're
- Ⓑ Who
- Ⓒ What
- Ⓓ Why

17. I hurt _____ while I was moving some boxes.
- Ⓐ myself
- Ⓑ me
- Ⓒ you
- Ⓓ back

18. _____ to hear that. Are you okay?
- Ⓐ You're sorry
- Ⓑ I'm sorry
- Ⓒ I'm glad
- Ⓓ You're glad

Yes. I'm okay.

Good.

10 Ⓐ Ⓑ Ⓒ Ⓓ	13 Ⓐ Ⓑ Ⓒ Ⓓ	16 Ⓐ Ⓑ Ⓒ Ⓓ
11 Ⓐ Ⓑ Ⓒ Ⓓ	14 Ⓐ Ⓑ Ⓒ Ⓓ	17 Ⓐ Ⓑ Ⓒ Ⓓ
12 Ⓐ Ⓑ Ⓒ Ⓓ	15 Ⓐ Ⓑ Ⓒ Ⓓ	18 Ⓐ Ⓑ Ⓒ Ⓓ

Go to the next page

Name ______________________________ Date ______________

C GRAMMAR IN CONTEXT: Oral Directions to Places; Clarification Strategies

Choose the correct answer to complete the conversations.

Ex: Excuse me. _____ the post office?

- Ⓐ Can I get
- Ⓑ Where can I
- Ⓒ How can
- ● How can I get to

19. Walk to the end of this block and _____ right.

- Ⓐ make
- Ⓑ have
- Ⓒ turn
- Ⓓ get

20. Can you tell me _____ Garden Street?

- Ⓐ how to get
- Ⓑ how to get to
- Ⓒ how you go
- Ⓓ how I go

21. Go _____ one block, turn left, and then _____ your second right.

- Ⓐ straight . . . make
- Ⓑ straight . . . turn
- Ⓒ street . . . take
- Ⓓ street . . . turn

22. Straight, left, and then the second _____ ?

- Ⓐ take
- Ⓑ straight
- Ⓒ left
- Ⓓ right

23. Yes. _____

- Ⓐ I'm correct.
- Ⓑ You're wrong.
- Ⓒ That's correct.
- Ⓓ That's incorrect.

24. Take Bus Number 7 and _____ at Lake Street.

- Ⓐ take off
- Ⓑ get on
- Ⓒ get off
- Ⓓ take on

25. _____ Bus Number 11?

- Ⓐ Did you say
- Ⓑ You say
- Ⓒ Do you say
- Ⓓ Did I say

26. _____ Number 7.

- Ⓐ Yes.
- Ⓑ No.
- Ⓒ Maybe.
- Ⓓ You say.

27. And _____ should I get off?

- Ⓐ who
- Ⓑ why
- Ⓒ how
- Ⓓ where

At Lake Street.

Thank you.

19	Ⓐ Ⓑ Ⓒ Ⓓ	22	Ⓐ Ⓑ Ⓒ Ⓓ	25	Ⓐ Ⓑ Ⓒ Ⓓ
20	Ⓐ Ⓑ Ⓒ Ⓓ	23	Ⓐ Ⓑ Ⓒ Ⓓ	26	Ⓐ Ⓑ Ⓒ Ⓓ
21	Ⓐ Ⓑ Ⓒ Ⓓ	24	Ⓐ Ⓑ Ⓒ Ⓓ	27	Ⓐ Ⓑ Ⓒ Ⓓ

Go to the next page

D READING: A Traffic Accident

Here is part of an accident report that describes an accident between two motor vehicles. Study the diagram and read the statement. Then do Numbers 28 through 31.

REPORT OF TRAFFIC ACCIDENT

9 - DIAGRAM

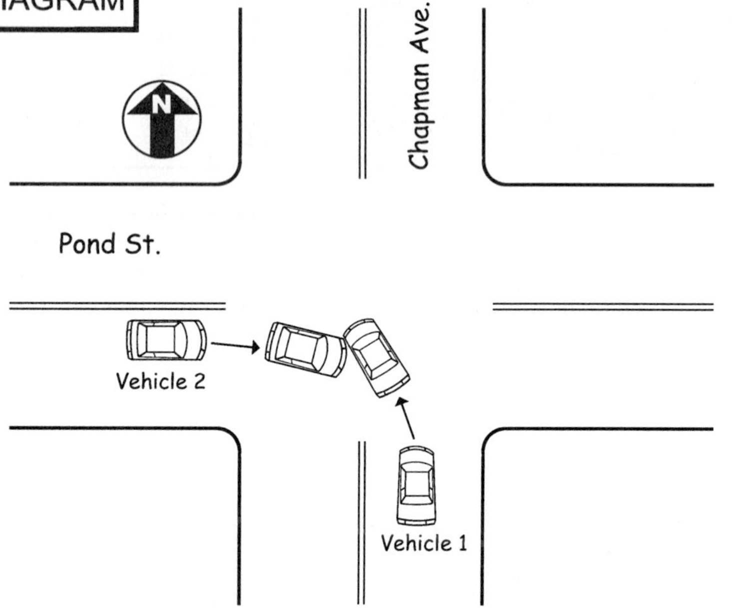

WEATHER CONDITIONS

01 Clear
02 Cloudy
03 Fog
04 Rain
05 Snow

01

ROAD SURFACE

01 Dry
02 Wet
03 Slippery
04 Icy

01

LIGHT CONDITIONS

01 Dawn
02 Daylight
03 Dusk
04 Dark

02

DESCRIBE WHAT HAPPENED:

I was driving north on Chapman Avenue. Vehicle 2 was going east on Pond Street. While I was making a left turn onto Pond Street, the driver of Vehicle 2 didn't stop at the Stop sign and hit the front left side of my car.

28. Where did this accident happen?

- (A) On Pond Street.
- (B) On Chapman Avenue.
- (C) While Vehicle 1 was turning left.
- (D) At the intersection of Pond and Chapman.

29. Where did Vehicle 2 hit Vehicle 1?

- (A) At the front right side.
- (B) At the back right side.
- (C) At the driver's side in the front.
- (D) At the driver's side in the back.

30. Where did the driver of Vehicle 1 want to go?

- (A) West on Pond Street.
- (B) East on Pond Street.
- (C) North on Pond Street.
- (D) South on Chapman Avenue.

31. When the police officer arrived, which driver probably received a ticket for a traffic violation?

- (A) The driver of Vehicle 1.
- (B) The driver of Vehicle 2.
- (C) Both drivers.
- (D) Neither driver.

28 (A) (B) (C) (D) 30 (A) (B) (C) (D)

29 (A) (B) (C) (D) 31 (A) (B) (C) (D)

Go to the next page

Name ______________________________ Date ______________

E CLOZE READING: Traffic

Choose the correct answers to complete the story.

I [arrived ● / get (B) / go (C)] at work late yesterday. I usually [drove (A) / drive (B) / went (C)] 32 on the Jackson Parkway to get to work, but there was bad [cars (A) / slow (B) / traffic (C)] 33 on the parkway yesterday. Instead, I [drive (A) / drove (B) / take (C)] 34 to work on Central Avenue. Unfortunately, there was a bad [accident (A) / traffic (B) / road (C)] 35 on Central Avenue. Traffic [doesn't (A) / didn't (B) / isn't (C)] 36 move for about an hour [where (A) / who (B) / while (C)] 37 the police helped the people in the accident.

F LISTENING ASSESSMENT: Following Directions to a Place

Read and listen to the questions. Then listen to the telephone conversation and answer the questions.

38. What is Rosa's address?
   - (A) 4013 Lake Street.
   - (B) 1430 Lake Street.
   - (C) 1430 Madison Street.
   - (D) 4013 Madison Street.

39. Where is David during this conversation?
   - (A) On Bus Number 5.
   - (B) At Rosa's party.
   - (C) At the post office.
   - (D) At an intersection.

40. Why did David get lost?
   - (A) He took the wrong bus.
   - (B) He got off the bus at the wrong street.
   - (C) He walked the wrong way on Lake Street.
   - (D) He walked the wrong way on Madison Street.

G LEARNING SKILL: Listing Events in Chronological Order

Put the events in order.

_____ I worked in my office all morning.
_____ I went home at 6 P.M.
_____ I went to a meeting in the afternoon.
__1__ I got dressed and had breakfast.
_____ I had lunch at noon.
_____ I took the bus to work.

32 (A) (B) (C) (D)   35 (A) (B) (C) (D)   38 (A) (B) (C) (D)
33 (A) (B) (C) (D)   36 (A) (B) (C) (D)   39 (A) (B) (C) (D)
34 (A) (B) (C) (D)   37 (A) (B) (C) (D)   40 (A) (B) (C) (D)

Go to the next page

H WRITING ASSESSMENT: A Traffic Accident Report Form

Imagine that you and another student were in a traffic accident. You were driving Vehicle 1. The other student was driving Vehicle 2. Work together to decide what happened and where. Then work separately to draw a diagram and write a statement about the accident. Finally, exchange information to complete the accident report.

REPORT OF TRAFFIC ACCIDENT

DIAGRAM (Draw a diagram of what happened.)

WEATHER CONDITIONS	ROAD SURFACE	LIGHT CONDITIONS
01 Clear 02 Cloudy 03 Fog 04 Rain 05 Snow ☐	01 Dry 02 Wet 03 Slippery 04 Icy ☐	01 Dawn 02 Daylight 03 Dusk 04 Dark ☐

DESCRIBE WHAT HAPPENED:

I SPEAKING ASSESSMENT

I can ask and answer these questions:

Ask	Answer	
☐	☐	What did you do yesterday?
☐	☐	What did you do last weekend?

Ask	Answer	
☐	☐	How did you get to school today?
☐	☐	How can I get to your home from here?

STOP

Name ______________________

Date ______________ Class ______________

3

A COMMUNICATING WITH SCHOOL PERSONNEL

Choose the correct answer.

1. _____ will the parents' meeting start this evening?
   - Ⓐ What day
   - Ⓑ What time
   - Ⓒ What day is it
   - Ⓓ What time is it

2. _____ give this note to my daughter's teacher?
   - Ⓐ You will
   - Ⓑ Please you will
   - Ⓒ You will please
   - Ⓓ Will you please

3. I promise _____ my daughter with her homework.
   - Ⓐ help
   - Ⓑ you help
   - Ⓒ I'll help
   - Ⓓ you'll help

4. _____ school tomorrow?
   - Ⓐ Will there be
   - Ⓑ Will be
   - Ⓒ Will open
   - Ⓓ Will be open

5. Could I _____ a pencil to fill out this form?
   - Ⓐ has
   - Ⓑ give
   - Ⓒ borrow
   - Ⓓ lend

6. Would you _____ me a textbook during the summer so I can help my son with math?
   - Ⓐ take
   - Ⓑ lend
   - Ⓒ read
   - Ⓓ borrow

7. Is Anthony _____ fail math this year?
   - Ⓐ going
   - Ⓑ going to
   - Ⓒ will
   - Ⓓ will be

8. _____ help me fill out this registration form?
   - Ⓐ Could you
   - Ⓑ Could I
   - Ⓒ Will I
   - Ⓓ Would we

9. _____ is my daughter doing in your class?
   - Ⓐ Why
   - Ⓑ When
   - Ⓒ Where
   - Ⓓ How

10. In my _____, the students aren't getting enough homework.
    - Ⓐ think
    - Ⓑ thinks
    - Ⓒ opinion
    - Ⓓ I think

11. My son _____ be in school tomorrow. _____ absent.
    - Ⓐ will . . . He's
    - Ⓑ will . . . He'll be
    - Ⓒ won't . . . He's
    - Ⓓ won't . . . He'll be

12. I think my son _____ doing his homework well because he _____ understand the assignments.
    - Ⓐ is . . . doesn't
    - Ⓑ isn't . . . doesn't
    - Ⓒ is . . . don't
    - Ⓓ isn't . . . does

1 Ⓐ Ⓑ Ⓒ Ⓓ	4 Ⓐ Ⓑ Ⓒ Ⓓ	7 Ⓐ Ⓑ Ⓒ Ⓓ	10 Ⓐ Ⓑ Ⓒ Ⓓ
2 Ⓐ Ⓑ Ⓒ Ⓓ	5 Ⓐ Ⓑ Ⓒ Ⓓ	8 Ⓐ Ⓑ Ⓒ Ⓓ	11 Ⓐ Ⓑ Ⓒ Ⓓ
3 Ⓐ Ⓑ Ⓒ Ⓓ	6 Ⓐ Ⓑ Ⓒ Ⓓ	9 Ⓐ Ⓑ Ⓒ Ⓓ	12 Ⓐ Ⓑ Ⓒ Ⓓ

Go to the next page

B GRAMMAR IN CONTEXT: Communicating with School Personnel—Reporting an Absence & Making an Appointment

Choose the correct answer to complete the conversations.

Good morning. Franklin Elementary School.

13. Hello. _____ Peter Chen.
  - Ⓐ This is
  - Ⓑ I
  - Ⓒ You
  - Ⓓ You are

Yes, Mr. Chen?

14. My son, Jason, is sick. He'll be _____ today.
  - Ⓐ a clinic
  - Ⓑ a doctor
  - Ⓒ absent
  - Ⓓ present

15. What's _____ teacher's name?
  - Ⓐ my
  - Ⓑ your
  - Ⓒ her
  - Ⓓ his

16. He's in Mrs. Tyler's _____ class.
  - Ⓐ four
  - Ⓑ fourth grade
  - Ⓒ grade
  - Ⓓ room

17. Hello. This is Sonia Belkin. I'd like to _____ with the principal.
  - Ⓐ make an appointment
  - Ⓑ appoint
  - Ⓒ appointment
  - Ⓓ meeting

18. Yes, Mrs. Belkin. Can you _____ tomorrow at 9 A.M.?
  - Ⓐ go
  - Ⓑ go out
  - Ⓒ come in
  - Ⓓ appointment

19. No. _____ working. How about the day after tomorrow?
  - Ⓐ You're
  - Ⓑ I
  - Ⓒ I'll
  - Ⓓ I'll be

20. I'm sorry. Mr. Price _____ be here. _____ at a meeting.
  - Ⓐ will . . . He'll be
  - Ⓑ won't . . . He'll be
  - Ⓒ will . . . He'll
  - Ⓓ won't . . . He'll

21. Can I _____ with him next Monday morning?
  - Ⓐ meet
  - Ⓑ meeting
  - Ⓒ appoint
  - Ⓓ appointment

22. Yes. _____ 10:00 okay?
  - Ⓐ Will
  - Ⓑ Be
  - Ⓒ Meet
  - Ⓓ Is

Yes. Thank you.

See you Monday, Mrs. Belkin.

13 Ⓐ Ⓑ Ⓒ Ⓓ
14 Ⓐ Ⓑ Ⓒ Ⓓ
15 Ⓐ Ⓑ Ⓒ Ⓓ
16 Ⓐ Ⓑ Ⓒ Ⓓ
17 Ⓐ Ⓑ Ⓒ Ⓓ
18 Ⓐ Ⓑ Ⓒ Ⓓ
19 Ⓐ Ⓑ Ⓒ Ⓓ
20 Ⓐ Ⓑ Ⓒ Ⓓ
21 Ⓐ Ⓑ Ⓒ Ⓓ
22 Ⓐ Ⓑ Ⓒ Ⓓ

Go to the next page

Name ____________________ Date ____________

C READING: A School Diagram

Here is a diagram of one floor of a high school. Study the diagram. Then do Numbers 23 through 30.

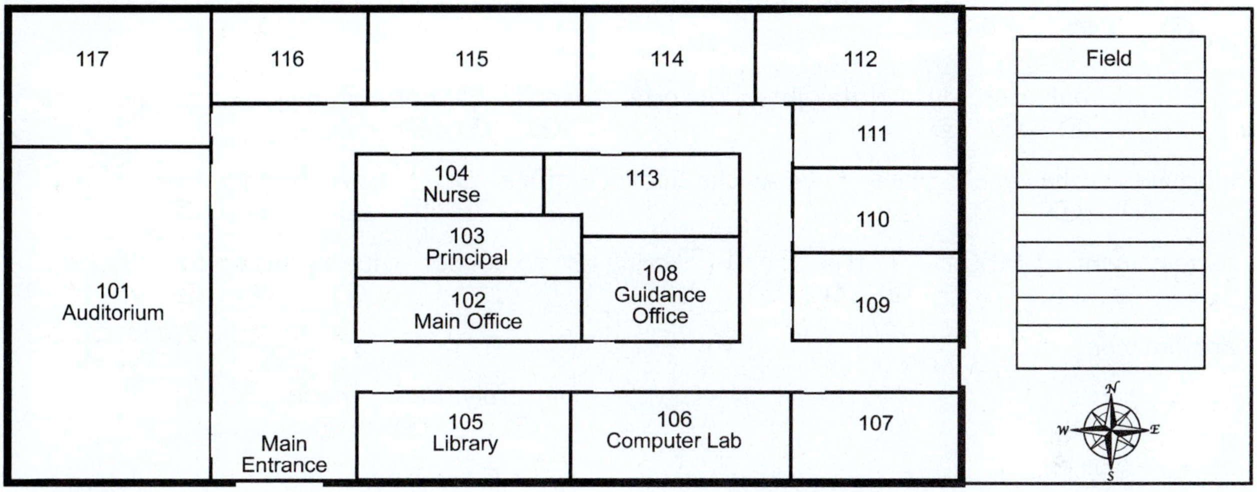

23. What's across from the main office?
- Ⓐ The gym.
- Ⓑ The guidance office.
- Ⓒ The library.
- Ⓓ The computer lab.

24. The music classroom is behind the auditorium. What's the music teacher's room number?
- Ⓐ 114.
- Ⓑ 115.
- Ⓒ 116.
- Ⓓ 117.

25. Where is the school's field?
- Ⓐ On the east side.
- Ⓑ On the west side.
- Ⓒ On the south side.
- Ⓓ On the north side.

26. Irene needs advice about her college applications. Where is she probably going?
- Ⓐ To Room 102.
- Ⓑ To Room 105.
- Ⓒ To Room 106.
- Ⓓ To Room 108.

27. Carlos doesn't feel well. Where is he probably going?
- Ⓐ To Room 104.
- Ⓑ To Room 103.
- Ⓒ To Room 102.
- Ⓓ To Room 101.

28. The cafeteria in this school is in Room 10. Where is it probably located?
- Ⓐ In the auditorium.
- Ⓑ In the basement.
- Ⓒ On the first floor.
- Ⓓ On the second floor.

29. Ms. Martin's classroom is Room Number 233. Where is it probably located?
- Ⓐ In the basement.
- Ⓑ On the first floor.
- Ⓒ On the second floor.
- Ⓓ On the third floor.

30. Which of these classrooms probably doesn't have any windows?
- Ⓐ Room 109.
- Ⓑ Room 111.
- Ⓒ Room 113.
- Ⓓ Room 115.

23 Ⓐ Ⓑ Ⓒ Ⓓ 25 Ⓐ Ⓑ Ⓒ Ⓓ 27 Ⓐ Ⓑ Ⓒ Ⓓ 29 Ⓐ Ⓑ Ⓒ Ⓓ

24 Ⓐ Ⓑ Ⓒ Ⓓ 26 Ⓐ Ⓑ Ⓒ Ⓓ 28 Ⓐ Ⓑ Ⓒ Ⓓ 30 Ⓐ Ⓑ Ⓒ Ⓓ

Go to the next page

D CLOZE READING: A Note to School

Choose the correct answers to complete the note.

Dare Ⓐ / Dear ● / Deer Ⓒ Ms. Watson,

Your Ⓐ / Her Ⓑ / My Ⓒ [31] daughter, Victoria, won't Ⓐ / will Ⓑ / not Ⓒ [32] be in school tomorrow morning. She Ⓐ / She'll Ⓑ / She's Ⓒ [33] be at the doctor's office. She have Ⓐ / has to Ⓑ / has Ⓒ [34] an appointment at 9:30. I Ⓐ / I'll Ⓑ / She'll Ⓒ [35] bring her to school during Ⓐ / after Ⓑ / for Ⓒ [36] the appointment.

Sincerely Ⓐ / Dear Ⓑ / Thank Ⓒ [37],

Lydia Petrero

E LISTENING ASSESSMENT: Communicating with School Personnel

Read and listen to the questions. Then listen to the telephone conversation and answer the questions.

38. Who is sick?
    - Ⓐ Raymond Vacano.
    - Ⓑ Mrs. Vacano.
    - Ⓒ The school nurse.
    - Ⓓ The gym teacher.

39. Where is the student now?
    - Ⓐ At home.
    - Ⓑ In the gym.
    - Ⓒ In the main office.
    - Ⓓ In the nurse's office.

40. Where should the mother go?
    - Ⓐ To the gym.
    - Ⓑ To the hospital.
    - Ⓒ To the nurse's office.
    - Ⓓ To the main office.

F WRITING ASSESSMENT: A Note to a Teacher

Write a note to your teacher. Explain why you will be absent during your next English class. (Use a separate sheet of paper.)

G SPEAKING ASSESSMENT: Small Talk about Weekend Plans

I can ask and answer these questions:

Ask	Answer	
☐	☐	What are you going to do this Saturday?
☐	☐	What are you going to do this Sunday?
☐	☐	What's the weather forecast for the weekend?

31 Ⓐ Ⓑ Ⓒ Ⓓ
32 Ⓐ Ⓑ Ⓒ Ⓓ
33 Ⓐ Ⓑ Ⓒ Ⓓ
34 Ⓐ Ⓑ Ⓒ Ⓓ
35 Ⓐ Ⓑ Ⓒ Ⓓ
36 Ⓐ Ⓑ Ⓒ Ⓓ
37 Ⓐ Ⓑ Ⓒ Ⓓ
38 Ⓐ Ⓑ Ⓒ Ⓓ
39 Ⓐ Ⓑ Ⓒ Ⓓ
40 Ⓐ Ⓑ Ⓒ Ⓓ

STOP

Name ____________________

Date ____________________ Class ____________________

4

A ASKING & ANSWERING TYPICAL JOB INTERVIEW QUESTIONS

Choose the correct answer.

1. Do you know how to _____ a bus?
   - (A) drive
   - (B) drives
   - (C) drove
   - (D) driven

2. I've _____ reports for many years.
   - (A) write
   - (B) writes
   - (C) wrote
   - (D) written

3. Have you ever _____ a presentation?
   - (A) give
   - (B) given
   - (C) gave
   - (D) gives

4. _____ you able to work weekends?
   - (A) Was
   - (B) Do
   - (C) Are
   - (D) Can

5. I know how to _____ inventory.
   - (A) took
   - (B) take
   - (C) taken
   - (D) takes

6. Have you ever _____ arrested?
   - (A) is
   - (B) was
   - (C) be
   - (D) been

7. I can _____ three languages.
   - (A) speak
   - (B) spoke
   - (C) speaks
   - (D) spoken

8. I _____ a computer class last year.
   - (A) take
   - (B) takes
   - (C) took
   - (D) taken

9. What _____ you do in your previous job?
   - (A) do
   - (B) did
   - (C) does
   - (D) done

10. Have you ever _____ a truck?
    - (A) drive
    - (B) drove
    - (C) drives
    - (D) driven

B SMALL TALK ABOUT LEISURE ACTIVITIES

11. A. Have you ever _____ skiing?
    B. Yes. I _____ skiing last year.
    - (A) went . . . go
    - (B) went . . . went
    - (C) gone . . . went
    - (D) go . . . went

12. A. Have you _____ the new Harry Potter movie yet?
    B. Yes. I _____ it last weekend.
    - (A) seen . . . saw
    - (B) saw . . . saw
    - (C) see . . . seen
    - (D) seen . . . see

13. A. I _____ to the mountains last Sunday.
    B. I've never _____ to the mountains.
    - (A) driven . . . drove
    - (B) driven . . . driven
    - (C) drove . . . drove
    - (D) drove . . . driven

14. A. Are you going to _____ today?
    B. No. I've already _____ this week.
    - (A) swim . . . swam
    - (B) swim . . . swum
    - (C) swum . . . swum
    - (D) swam . . . swim

1	(A)	(B)	(C)	(D)
2	(A)	(B)	(C)	(D)
3	(A)	(B)	(C)	(D)
4	(A)	(B)	(C)	(D)
5	(A)	(B)	(C)	(D)
6	(A)	(B)	(C)	(D)
7	(A)	(B)	(C)	(D)
8	(A)	(B)	(C)	(D)
9	(A)	(B)	(C)	(D)
10	(A)	(B)	(C)	(D)
11	(A)	(B)	(C)	(D)
12	(A)	(B)	(C)	(D)
13	(A)	(B)	(C)	(D)
14	(A)	(B)	(C)	(D)

Go to the next page

C GRAMMAR IN CONTEXT: Job Interview

15. Do you know how to _____ X-rays?
   - (A) take
   - (B) takes
   - (C) took
   - (D) taken

16. Yes. I've _____ X-rays for many years.
   - (A) take
   - (B) takes
   - (C) took
   - (D) taken

17. Where _____ you work now?
   - (A) does
   - (B) do
   - (C) done
   - (D) did

18. _____ work at the Midtown Clinic.
   - (A) I
   - (B) I'm
   - (C) I've
   - (D) I'll

19. _____ you worked there for a long time?
   - (A) Do
   - (B) Did
   - (C) Have
   - (D) Has

20. Yes. _____ worked there for many years.
   - (A) I
   - (B) I'm
   - (C) I've
   - (D) I did

D GRAMMAR IN CONTEXT: Following a Sequence of Instructions; Organizing Tasks

21. First, _____ the paychecks from the payroll office.
   - (A) get
   - (B) got
   - (C) gets
   - (D) gotten

22. I've already _____ them.
   - (A) get
   - (B) got
   - (C) gets
   - (D) gotten

23. Then _____ the paychecks to the mailroom.
   - (A) took
   - (B) take
   - (C) taken
   - (D) takes

24. I've _____ them there already.
   - (A) took
   - (B) take
   - (C) taken
   - (D) takes

25. Finally, _____ the paychecks in each employee's mailbox.
   - (A) put
   - (B) puts
   - (C) have put
   - (D) did put

26. I haven't _____ that yet, but I'll _____ it right away.
   - (A) do . . . do
   - (B) did . . . do
   - (C) done . . . do
   - (D) done . . . doing

15 (A) (B) (C) (D)	18 (A) (B) (C) (D)	21 (A) (B) (C) (D)	24 (A) (B) (C) (D)
16 (A) (B) (C) (D)	19 (A) (B) (C) (D)	22 (A) (B) (C) (D)	25 (A) (B) (C) (D)
17 (A) (B) (C) (D)	20 (A) (B) (C) (D)	23 (A) (B) (C) (D)	26 (A) (B) (C) (D)

Go to the next page

Name ______________________ Date ____________

E CLOZE READING: Employment Application Procedures

Choose the correct answers to complete the story.

I've completed my job [applying (A) / application (B, marked) / employer (C)] form. I've filled in all my personal [application (A) / vocation (B) / information (C)][27] I've stated the [position (A) / company (B) / employee (C)][28] I'm applying for. I've listed my high school and college in the [work (A) / education (B) / application (C)][29] history. I've listed my [now (A) / today (B) / current (C)][30] and former jobs. I've written my [days (A) / dates (B) / schedules (C)][31] of employment for each position. I've written the name and address of each [employer (A) / employee (B) / employment (C)][32]. I've given the [explain (A) / excuse (B) / reason (C)][33] for leaving each position. I've given the names of three [applications (A) / references (B) / addresses (C)][34]. I've described all my [skills (A) / works (B) / job (C)][35], including languages I [know (A) / can (B) / how (C)][36] speak. I've [correct (A) / listed (B) / checked (C)][37] the application to make sure it is complete.

F LISTENING ASSESSMENT: A Job Interview

Read and listen to the questions. Then listen to the job interview and answer the questions.

38. Where is the job interview probably taking place?
- (A) At a supermarket.
- (B) In a restaurant.
- (C) At a school.
- (D) In a department store.

39. When CAN'T the job applicant work?
- (A) Mornings.
- (B) Afternoons.
- (C) Evenings.
- (D) Weekends.

40. How often are the employees paid?
- (A) Once a year.
- (B) Once a month.
- (C) Once a week.
- (D) Once a day.

27 (A) (B) (C) (D)	31 (A) (B) (C) (D)	35 (A) (B) (C) (D)	39 (A) (B) (C) (D)
28 (A) (B) (C) (D)	32 (A) (B) (C) (D)	36 (A) (B) (C) (D)	40 (A) (B) (C) (D)
29 (A) (B) (C) (D)	33 (A) (B) (C) (D)	37 (A) (B) (C) (D)	
30 (A) (B) (C) (D)	34 (A) (B) (C) (D)	38 (A) (B) (C) (D)	

Go to the next page

G WRITING ASSESSMENT: A Job Application Form

Complete the job application form. (Use any information you wish.)

PERSONAL INFORMATION

NAME ______________________________ SOCIAL SECURITY NUMBER ______________
LAST FIRST MIDDLE

ADDRESS ______________________________ TELEPHONE ______________
NUMBER STREET CITY STATE ZIP CODE

EDUCATION HISTORY

HIGH SCHOOL ______________________________ DIPLOMA OR GED RECEIVED: ___ YES ___ NO DATE ______
NAME CITY STATE

COLLEGE/VOCATIONAL SCHOOL

NAME	LOCATION	FIELD OF STUDY	DEGREE/CERTIFICATION	DATE

EMPLOYMENT HISTORY (List most recent first.)

Date	Name & Address of Employer	Position	Salary	Name of Supervisor	Reason for Leaving
From: To:					
Duties					
From: To:					
Duties					
From: To:					
Duties					

SKILLS

LIST ANY SPECIAL TRAINING OR SKILLS YOU HAVE

____

____

SIGNATURE ______________________________ DATE ______________

H SPEAKING ASSESSMENT

I can ask and answer these questions:

Ask	Answer	
☐	☐	Do you know how to ________?
☐	☐	Have you seen *title of movie*?
☐	☐	What have you already done today?
☐	☐	What haven't you done yet?

STOP

Name ______________________________

Date ______________ Class ______________

5

A GIVING PERSONAL INFORMATION ABOUT SELF, FAMILY, & JOB HISTORY

Example:

How long have you _____ a mechanic?
- Ⓐ are
- Ⓑ were
- Ⓒ be
- ● been

1. Have you always _____ here in Miami?
   - Ⓐ live
   - Ⓑ lived
   - Ⓒ living
   - Ⓓ you lived

2. How long have you _____ how to fix computers?
   - Ⓐ know
   - Ⓑ knew
   - Ⓒ known
   - Ⓓ knows

3. I've been a taxi driver _____ three years.
   - Ⓐ for
   - Ⓑ since
   - Ⓒ during
   - Ⓓ with

4. My family has lived here _____ 2001.
   - Ⓐ until
   - Ⓑ since
   - Ⓒ before
   - Ⓓ for

5. I've known how to speak French _____ a child.
   - Ⓐ for I'm
   - Ⓑ for I was
   - Ⓒ since I'm
   - Ⓓ since I was

6. Have you been a carpenter _____ a long time?
   - Ⓐ for
   - Ⓑ when
   - Ⓒ ago
   - Ⓓ since

7. _____ worked in my current job since May. Before that, _____ worked at a supermarket.
   - Ⓐ I . . . I
   - Ⓑ I . . . I've
   - Ⓒ I've . . . I
   - Ⓓ I've . . . I've

B STATING SKILLS, QUALIFICATIONS, & PERSONAL QUALITIES

Example:

I _____ type, file, and use a computer.
- Ⓐ known how
- Ⓑ known how to
- Ⓒ know how
- ● know how to

8. I _____.
   - Ⓐ hard work
   - Ⓑ harder work
   - Ⓒ work hard
   - Ⓓ am hard work

9. I have a lot of _____.
   - Ⓐ experience
   - Ⓑ employment
   - Ⓒ qualification
   - Ⓓ job

10. I'm never late. I'm very _____.
    - Ⓐ on time
    - Ⓑ for work
    - Ⓒ out of time
    - Ⓓ punctual

1 Ⓐ Ⓑ Ⓒ Ⓓ	4 Ⓐ Ⓑ Ⓒ Ⓓ	7 Ⓐ Ⓑ Ⓒ Ⓓ	9 Ⓐ Ⓑ Ⓒ Ⓓ
2 Ⓐ Ⓑ Ⓒ Ⓓ	5 Ⓐ Ⓑ Ⓒ Ⓓ	8 Ⓐ Ⓑ Ⓒ Ⓓ	10 Ⓐ Ⓑ Ⓒ Ⓓ
3 Ⓐ Ⓑ Ⓒ Ⓓ	6 Ⓐ Ⓑ Ⓒ Ⓓ		

Go to the next page

C GRAMMAR IN CONTEXT: Job Interview

Example:

_____ you working now?

- Ⓐ Will
- ● Are
- Ⓒ Have
- Ⓓ Do

11. Yes, I _____.
- Ⓐ do
- Ⓑ can
- Ⓒ am
- Ⓓ will

12. Where _____ you work now?
- Ⓐ have
- Ⓑ is
- Ⓒ did
- Ⓓ do

13. _____ at Tops Office Supplies.
- Ⓐ I work
- Ⓑ I worked
- Ⓒ I've worked
- Ⓓ I'll work

14. How long _____ there?
- Ⓐ do you work
- Ⓑ have you worked
- Ⓒ did you work
- Ⓓ does your work

15. _____ there since January.
- Ⓐ I work
- Ⓑ I worked
- Ⓒ I've worked
- Ⓓ I'll work

16. Where _____ before that?
- Ⓐ did you work
- Ⓑ have worked
- Ⓒ do you work
- Ⓓ you work

17. _____ at Shay's Supermarket.
- Ⓐ I work
- Ⓑ I'll work
- Ⓒ I've worked
- Ⓓ I worked

18. How long _____ there?
- Ⓐ you work
- Ⓑ do you work
- Ⓒ did you work
- Ⓓ have you worked

19. _____ two years.
- Ⓐ From
- Ⓑ For
- Ⓒ During
- Ⓓ Since

11 Ⓐ Ⓑ Ⓒ Ⓓ　14 Ⓐ Ⓑ Ⓒ Ⓓ　16 Ⓐ Ⓑ Ⓒ Ⓓ　18 Ⓐ Ⓑ Ⓒ Ⓓ

12 Ⓐ Ⓑ Ⓒ Ⓓ　15 Ⓐ Ⓑ Ⓒ Ⓓ　17 Ⓐ Ⓑ Ⓒ Ⓓ　19 Ⓐ Ⓑ Ⓒ Ⓓ

13 Ⓐ Ⓑ Ⓒ Ⓓ

Go to the next page

Name ______________________________ Date ____________

D GRAMMAR IN CONTEXT: Clarifying to Ask for Meaning

Example:
How long have you ____ unemployed?
- Ⓐ be
- ● been
- Ⓒ are
- Ⓓ was

20. I'm sorry. ____ does "unemployed" mean?
- Ⓐ Who
- Ⓑ What
- Ⓒ How
- Ⓓ Why

21. How long ____ out of work?
- Ⓐ you are
- Ⓑ you were
- Ⓒ have you been
- Ⓓ you have been

22. ____ two months.
- Ⓐ For
- Ⓑ Since
- Ⓒ With
- Ⓓ From

23. ____ you naturalized?
- Ⓐ Has
- Ⓑ Did
- Ⓒ Do
- Ⓓ Are

24. I'm sorry. What does that ____?
- Ⓐ say
- Ⓑ word
- Ⓒ mean
- Ⓓ understand

25. ____ you become a citizen yet?
- Ⓐ Do
- Ⓑ Are
- Ⓒ Has
- Ⓓ Have

26. Yes. ____ a citizen since 2003.
- Ⓐ I was
- Ⓑ I've been
- Ⓒ I'm not
- Ⓓ I have

27. ____ you ever been incarcerated?
- Ⓐ Have
- Ⓑ Did
- Ⓒ Were
- Ⓓ Was

28. I'm sorry. I don't ____ what that means.
- Ⓐ ask
- Ⓑ repeat
- Ⓒ understand
- Ⓓ sorry

Have you ever been in jail?

No, I haven't.

20 Ⓐ Ⓑ Ⓒ Ⓓ　23 Ⓐ Ⓑ Ⓒ Ⓓ　25 Ⓐ Ⓑ Ⓒ Ⓓ　27 Ⓐ Ⓑ Ⓒ Ⓓ
21 Ⓐ Ⓑ Ⓒ Ⓓ　24 Ⓐ Ⓑ Ⓒ Ⓓ　26 Ⓐ Ⓑ Ⓒ Ⓓ　28 Ⓐ Ⓑ Ⓒ Ⓓ
22 Ⓐ Ⓑ Ⓒ Ⓓ

Go to the next page

E READING: Job Ads

Look at the job advertisements. Then do Numbers 29 through 32.

SaveMart is now hiring!

- Full Time, Part Time, & Sunday Only Positions
- Flexible Hours & Schedules
- Excellent Salary & Benefits
- Store Employee Discount

Positions now available:

Sales • Cashiers • Security

Ask for an application at the Service Desk.

Join the Burger World Team!

- Free Meals
- Free Uniforms
- Promotion Opportunities
- Regular Wage Increases
- Academic Scholarships

Counter, Crew, & Manager positions available

CARPENTER
Exper. req. Must have tools & trans.
Call 564-9234.

DATA ENTRY CLERK
FT. Will train. Good math skills req.
$8/hr. Call 729-4444.

OFFICE ASST.
PT. M–F. 9am–1pm. Office exper. pref.
Call 426-8080.

29. Which job advertisement isn't in the newspaper?
- Ⓐ The ad for a carpenter.
- Ⓑ The ad for cashiers.
- Ⓒ The ad for an office assistant.
- Ⓓ The ad for a data entry clerk.

30. Which ad gives the best information about the salary?
- Ⓐ The ad for a salesperson.
- Ⓑ The ad for an office assistant.
- Ⓒ The ad for a carpenter.
- Ⓓ The ad for a data entry clerk.

31. Which statement about the office assistant position is NOT true?
- Ⓐ The position is part-time.
- Ⓑ The person will work 5 days a week.
- Ⓒ Experience is required.
- Ⓓ The person will work 20 hours a week.

32. Brenda already works full-time Monday through Friday. She wants to earn more money on weekends. Which job should she apply for?
- Ⓐ A job at SaveMart.
- Ⓑ A job at Burger World.
- Ⓒ The data entry clerk position.
- Ⓓ The office assistant position.

29 Ⓐ Ⓑ Ⓒ Ⓓ 30 Ⓐ Ⓑ Ⓒ Ⓓ 31 Ⓐ Ⓑ Ⓒ Ⓓ 32 Ⓐ Ⓑ Ⓒ Ⓓ

Go to the next page

Name ______________________ Date ______________

F GRAMMAR IN CONTEXT: Small Talk

Example:
_____ been?
Ⓐ Are you
Ⓑ How
● How have you
Ⓓ How you have

33. _____ fine, thanks.
Ⓐ I've been
Ⓑ You've been
Ⓒ You're
Ⓓ I

34. How long _____ your daughter lived in Portland?
Ⓐ is
Ⓑ has
Ⓒ was
Ⓓ did

35. She's lived there _____ two years.
Ⓐ since
Ⓑ during
Ⓒ in
Ⓓ for

36. How long _____ your wife?
Ⓐ you know
Ⓑ you knew
Ⓒ has
Ⓓ have you known

37. I've known her since _____ in high school.
Ⓐ we were
Ⓑ we are
Ⓒ we're
Ⓓ she's

G LISTENING ASSESSMENT: Responding to a Job Ad; Abbreviations

Read and listen to the questions. Then listen to the conversation and answer the questions.

38. Which abbreviation describes the hours for this position?
Ⓐ PT
Ⓑ FT
Ⓒ Flexible hrs.
Ⓓ 8 hrs./wk.

39. Which statement describes the experience this job requires?
Ⓐ Excel. benefits
Ⓑ Typing skills pref.
Ⓒ Office exper. req.
Ⓓ Office exper. pref.

40. Which sentence is probably in the ad for this job?
Ⓐ No calls.
Ⓑ Apply in person.
Ⓒ Call Pat at 421-2000.
Ⓓ Ask for Pat at the service counter.

33 Ⓐ Ⓑ Ⓒ Ⓓ   35 Ⓐ Ⓑ Ⓒ Ⓓ   37 Ⓐ Ⓑ Ⓒ Ⓓ   39 Ⓐ Ⓑ Ⓒ Ⓓ
34 Ⓐ Ⓑ Ⓒ Ⓓ   36 Ⓐ Ⓑ Ⓒ Ⓓ   38 Ⓐ Ⓑ Ⓒ Ⓓ   40 Ⓐ Ⓑ Ⓒ Ⓓ

Go to the next page

H WRITING ASSESSMENT: A Resume

Write a resume. List your work experience, your education history, and your skills (languages you speak, computer skills, machines you can operate, licenses you have).

(Name)

(Address)

(Phone Number or E-mail)

WORK EXPERIENCE (LIST MOST RECENT FIRST)

Dates — Position, Place of Employment

City, State

Description of job duties

Dates — Position, Place of Employment

City, State

Description of job duties

Dates — Position, Place of Employment

City, State

Description of job duties

EDUCATION HISTORY

Dates — Degree or certificate

School, City, State

Dates — Degree or certificate

School, City, State

SKILLS

I SPEAKING ASSESSMENT

I can ask and answer these questions:

Ask	Answer	
☐	☐	Where do you live now?
☐	☐	How long have you lived there?
☐	☐	Where did you live before that?
☐	☐	How long did you live there?
☐	☐	Who is your best friend?
☐	☐	How long have you known her/him?
☐	☐	Who is the leader of your country?
☐	☐	How long has she/he been the leader?

STOP

Name ______________________________

Date ____________________ Class ____________________

6

A RENTING AN APARTMENT

Example:

How much is the ____?

● rent
Ⓑ landlord
Ⓒ utilities
Ⓓ tenant

1. A rental agreement is ____.
Ⓐ a landlord
Ⓑ a lease
Ⓒ a utility
Ⓓ rent

2. Are pets ____ in the building?
Ⓐ permitted
Ⓑ permission
Ⓒ may I
Ⓓ rules

3. ____ utilities included in the rent?
Ⓐ Do
Ⓑ Does
Ⓒ Are
Ⓓ Is

4. What are the ____ of the building?
Ⓐ don't
Ⓑ allowed
Ⓒ permitted
Ⓓ rules

5. Does the rent ____ a parking space?
Ⓐ include
Ⓑ allowed
Ⓒ have
Ⓓ garage

6. Throw trash in the ____.
Ⓐ hallway
Ⓑ dumpster
Ⓒ recycling bin
Ⓓ garbage disposal

7. If something is broken, fill out a ____ request form.
Ⓐ pest control
Ⓑ problem
Ⓒ maintenance
Ⓓ building

8. It is prohibited to hang laundry on the ____.
Ⓐ entrance
Ⓑ apartment
Ⓒ balcony
Ⓓ place

9. Make sure you understand a lease before you ____ it.
Ⓐ deposit
Ⓑ write
Ⓒ rent
Ⓓ sign

1 Ⓐ Ⓑ Ⓒ Ⓓ	4 Ⓐ Ⓑ Ⓒ Ⓓ	7 Ⓐ Ⓑ Ⓒ Ⓓ
2 Ⓐ Ⓑ Ⓒ Ⓓ	5 Ⓐ Ⓑ Ⓒ Ⓓ	8 Ⓐ Ⓑ Ⓒ Ⓓ
3 Ⓐ Ⓑ Ⓒ Ⓓ	6 Ⓐ Ⓑ Ⓒ Ⓓ	9 Ⓐ Ⓑ Ⓒ Ⓓ

Go to the next page

B GRAMMAR IN CONTEXT: Offering to Help; Working Cooperatively; Thanking Someone

Example:

You _____ tired.

- Ⓐ look (filled in)
- Ⓑ looks
- Ⓒ looking
- Ⓓ looked

10. I am. _____ washing windows since 9:00 this morning.

- Ⓐ I
- Ⓑ I've been
- Ⓒ I'm
- Ⓓ I'll

11. Really? How many windows _____?

- Ⓐ you wash
- Ⓑ you washed
- Ⓒ you have washed
- Ⓓ have you washed

12. _____ eight windows.

- Ⓐ I wash
- Ⓑ I'll wash
- Ⓒ I've washed
- Ⓓ you washed

13. Would you like me to _____?

- Ⓐ help you
- Ⓑ you help
- Ⓒ your help
- Ⓓ help me

14. Thanks. I _____.

- Ⓐ appreciate
- Ⓑ appreciate it
- Ⓒ thank
- Ⓓ grateful

15. What _____ doing?

- Ⓐ you been
- Ⓑ have been
- Ⓒ have you been
- Ⓓ you have been

16. _____ the closets.

- Ⓐ Clean
- Ⓑ I clean
- Ⓒ I'm going to clean
- Ⓓ I've been cleaning

17. _____ I can do to help?

- Ⓐ There's anything
- Ⓑ There's something
- Ⓒ Is anything there
- Ⓓ Is there anything

18. Yes. Please _____ these newspapers in the recycling bin.

- Ⓐ put
- Ⓑ will put
- Ⓒ have put
- Ⓓ you put

10 Ⓐ Ⓑ Ⓒ Ⓓ
11 Ⓐ Ⓑ Ⓒ Ⓓ
12 Ⓐ Ⓑ Ⓒ Ⓓ
13 Ⓐ Ⓑ Ⓒ Ⓓ
14 Ⓐ Ⓑ Ⓒ Ⓓ
15 Ⓐ Ⓑ Ⓒ Ⓓ
16 Ⓐ Ⓑ Ⓒ Ⓓ
17 Ⓐ Ⓑ Ⓒ Ⓓ
18 Ⓐ Ⓑ Ⓒ Ⓓ

Go to the next page

Name ______________________ Date ____________

C READING: Scanning a Utility Bill for Most Essential Information

Look at the utility bill. Then do Numbers 19 through 22.

California Power and Light
P.O. Box 3566
Los Angeles, CA 90016
Web address: www.cpl.com

Customer assistance line
1-800-555-7600
To report a power outage
1-800-555-3000

Account Number **235-12-55-78304**
Hector Nieves
15 Park Drive
Los Angeles, CA 90020

Billing Date: 11/15/10
Payment Due: 12/10/10
Next Meter Read Date: 12/14/10

Billing Summary

Amount of Previous Statement 10/15/10	$ 89.91
Payment Received— 11/09/10 Thank You	89.91
Balance Before Current Charges	0.00
Current Charges	96.45
Your Total Balance Due	$ 96.45

Your current energy usage

Meter Number	From	To	Usage
AB910731	10/14/10	11/14/10	
	51291	51905	614 kilowatt hours

Reminder — a 9% late payment will be added to the total unpaid balance of your account if a full payment is not received by the due date on this bill.

Please write your account number on your check.

19. This is ____.
- Ⓐ a telephone bill
- Ⓑ an electric bill
- Ⓒ a gas bill
- Ⓓ a cable TV bill

20. Mr. Nieves has to pay this bill on or before ____.
- Ⓐ November 14
- Ⓑ November 15
- Ⓒ December 10
- Ⓓ December 14

21. The total amount due now is ____.
- Ⓐ 614 kilowatt hours
- Ⓑ $0.00
- Ⓒ $89.91
- Ⓓ $96.45

22. When Mr. Nieves pays this bill, he should write the number ____ on the check.
- Ⓐ 235-12-55-78304
- Ⓑ 1-800-555-7600
- Ⓒ 1-800-555-3000
- Ⓓ AB910731

19 Ⓐ Ⓑ Ⓒ Ⓓ 20 Ⓐ Ⓑ Ⓒ Ⓓ 21 Ⓐ Ⓑ Ⓒ Ⓓ 22 Ⓐ Ⓑ Ⓒ Ⓓ

Go to the next page

D READING: Yellow Pages; Housing Maintenance & Repairs

Look at the yellow pages listings. Then do Numbers 23 through 26.

Painters—Plumbing 452

PAINTERS

see also Handymen, Home Improvement Services

D & K Painting —*See our ad previous page*
586 N 32 Mid 205 468–3498

Mike's Painting
Serving Marbury for Over 25 Years
www.mikepaint.com 334 457–2479

HARMONY PAINTERS —*See our ad this page*
1238 Main Mal 334 781–5908

RAMIREZ PAINTING INC.—*See our ad this page*
675 River May 205 672–3349

PEST CONTROL SPECIALISTS

Bugs–Away Pest Control
277 Summer Mal 334 468–1633

Modern Pest Services
1029 Market Mil 205 842–2567

PHARMACIES

Wall's Pharmacy
926 Tyler Mil 205 572–9050

PIZZA

ABC Pizza
10 Market May 205 672–4902

PLUMBING CONTRACTORS

AAA Plumbing Services
777 Harrison Mal 205 842–3310

CARTER'S PLUMBING AND HEATING —*See our ad on page 454*
1300 Franklin Mid 205 842–8061

JEFF'S PLUMBING AND HEATING INC. —*See our ad this page*
212 South Mil 205 468–2855

Harmony Painters
1238 Main Street, Malvern
Interior and Exterior
Smoke, Fire, and Water Damage Repair
Ask about our 5-year guarantee **334 781–5908**

Ramirez Painting Inc.
675 River Street, Maytown
Family-Owned Business
After-Hour Scheduling
205 672–3349
Receive 10% off labor when you mention this ad

Jeff's Plumbing and Heating Inc.
212 South Street, Millport
All Your Plumbing Needs
Tubs and Toilets
Water Heaters
Faucets and Sinks
Garbage Disposals
24-Hour Emergency Service
205 468–2855
SENIOR DISCOUNTS

23. You're looking for a painting company in Midfield. You should call ____.

Ⓐ 334 457-2479
Ⓑ 334 781-5908
Ⓒ 205 468-3498
Ⓓ 205 672-3349

24. There are roaches in your kitchen. You live in Malvern. You should call ____.

Ⓐ 334 457-2479
Ⓑ 334 468-1633
Ⓒ 205 842-2567
Ⓓ 205 572-9050

25. It's midnight. A pipe in your bathroom just broke. You should call ____.

Ⓐ 205 468-2855
Ⓑ 205 842-3310
Ⓒ 205 842-8061
Ⓓ 911

26. There isn't an ad for ____ on this page.

Ⓐ Harmony Painters
Ⓑ Jeff's Plumbing and Heating
Ⓒ Ramirez Painting
Ⓓ D & K Painting

23 Ⓐ Ⓑ Ⓒ Ⓓ 24 Ⓐ Ⓑ Ⓒ Ⓓ 25 Ⓐ Ⓑ Ⓒ Ⓓ 26 Ⓐ Ⓑ Ⓒ Ⓓ

Go to the next page

Name ______________________________ Date ______________

E CLOZE READING: Housing Maintenance & Repairs

Choose the correct answers to complete the notice to tenants in an apartment building.

To: All Tenants
From: Your Building [Maintenance (A) / Mandatory (B) / Manager (C) ●]

Please remember to follow these [reports (A) / rules (B) / requests (C)] 27 of the building:

Throw all trash in the [recycling bin (A) / dumpster (B) / hallway (C)] 28.

Put metal cans and [garbage (A) / landfill (B) / glass (C)] 29 in the recycling bins.

Don't forget: Recycling in our city is [mandatory (A) / waste (B) / routine (C)] 30.

Always turn on the water when you use the garbage [storage (A) / disposal (B) / bin (C)] 31.

Report any broken [pest (A) / kitchen (B) / smoke (C)] 32 detectors immediately.

Also report any other fire [safety (A) / hazards (B) / service (C)] 33.

Call the [rental (A) / storage (B) / common (C)] 34 office if you need the pest [collection (A) / control (B) / preparation (C)] 35 company.

Please do not call us with routine [maintenance (A) / emergency (B) / request (C)] 36 problems.

Fill out a maintenance request [program (A) / law (B) / form (C)] 37.

F LISTENING ASSESSMENT: Renting an Apartment

Read and listen to the questions. Then listen to the conversation and answer the questions.

38. Which pets are NOT allowed in the building?
- (A) Birds.
- (B) Small dogs.
- (C) Cats.
- (D) Large dogs.

39. Which utility is included in the rent?
- (A) Electricity.
- (B) Heat.
- (C) Cable TV.
- (D) Telephone.

40. Where can tenants park a second car?
- (A) In the parking lot.
- (B) In the garage.
- (C) In the rental office.
- (D) In the visitor parking spaces.

27 (A) (B) (C) (D)	31 (A) (B) (C) (D)	35 (A) (B) (C) (D)	39 (A) (B) (C) (D)
28 (A) (B) (C) (D)	32 (A) (B) (C) (D)	36 (A) (B) (C) (D)	40 (A) (B) (C) (D)
29 (A) (B) (C) (D)	33 (A) (B) (C) (D)	37 (A) (B) (C) (D)	
30 (A) (B) (C) (D)	34 (A) (B) (C) (D)	38 (A) (B) (C) (D)	

Go to the next page

G WRITING ASSESSMENT: Bank Transactions

Withdraw $200.00 from your savings account. Your account number is 83219745.

Deposit your paycheck for $575.25 in your account and get $100.00 in cash. Your account number is 42439182.

WITHDRAWAL APPLICATION Date ____________

____
Account number

CASH WITHDRAWAL	
CHECK WITHDRAWAL	
TOTAL WITHDRAWAL	

____
Signature

DEPOSIT SLIP Date ____________

____
Account number

____
Name

____
Sign here ONLY if cash received from deposit

CURRENCY	
COIN	
CHECKS	
LESS CASH	
TOTAL	

Fill out the check to pay this bill.

E-Star Energy

Electricity	$37.92
Past Due	0.00
DUE NOW	$37.92

1024

____

Pay to the order of ____________ $____________

____________ *Dollars*

For ____________ ____________

057009345 200042534 1024

Now record this check in the check register and calculate the new balance.

Number	Date	Description	Amount of Debit (–)	Amount of Credit (+)	Balance
1022	1/14	Metrovision Cable TV	49.50		1,461.50
1023	1/16	Telecom	32.51		1,428.99

H SPEAKING ASSESSMENT

I can ask and answer these questions:

Ask Answer

☐ ☐ What street do you live on?

☐ ☐ How long have you been living on that street?

☐ ☐ Where else have you lived?

Ask Answer

☐ ☐ How long have you been studying English?

☐ ☐ Have you ever had a maintenance or repair problem where you live? What happened?

STOP

Name ____________________

Date ____________ Class ____________

7

A REQUESTS AT WORK

Example:

Thank you ____ copying the report.
- Ⓐ with
- Ⓑ at
- Ⓒ the
- ● for

1. ____ clean the tables?
- Ⓐ Please you would
- Ⓑ Would please you
- Ⓒ Would you please
- Ⓓ Please would

2. Could I possibly ____ your pen?
- Ⓐ lend
- Ⓑ borrow
- Ⓒ lend me
- Ⓓ borrow you

3. Would you please ____ your calculator?
- Ⓐ borrow
- Ⓑ borrow me
- Ⓒ lend
- Ⓓ lend me

4. ____ happy to do it.
- Ⓐ I
- Ⓑ I be
- Ⓒ I'll be
- Ⓓ You

5. Thank you for ____ the chairs.
- Ⓐ setting up
- Ⓑ sets up
- Ⓒ set up
- Ⓓ you set up

6. ____ take the day off tomorrow?
- Ⓐ I'm possibly
- Ⓑ Could I possibly
- Ⓒ I could possibly
- Ⓓ Could possibly

7. Would you ____ help me with my presentation?
- Ⓐ possible
- Ⓑ can
- Ⓒ are able to
- Ⓓ be able to

8. I ____ take my son to a doctor's appointment tomorrow.
- Ⓐ have
- Ⓑ have to
- Ⓒ going
- Ⓓ going to

9. I'm asking for ____ tomorrow because my husband will be in the hospital.
- Ⓐ the day off
- Ⓑ the off day
- Ⓒ day off
- Ⓓ off day

1	Ⓐ	Ⓑ	Ⓒ	Ⓓ	4	Ⓐ	Ⓑ	Ⓒ	Ⓓ	7	Ⓐ	Ⓑ	Ⓒ	Ⓓ
2	Ⓐ	Ⓑ	Ⓒ	Ⓓ	5	Ⓐ	Ⓑ	Ⓒ	Ⓓ	8	Ⓐ	Ⓑ	Ⓒ	Ⓓ
3	Ⓐ	Ⓑ	Ⓒ	Ⓓ	6	Ⓐ	Ⓑ	Ⓒ	Ⓓ	9	Ⓐ	Ⓑ	Ⓒ	Ⓓ

Go to the next page

B GRAMMAR IN CONTEXT: Requests at Work; Small Talk at Work

Example:

_____ set up the tables and chairs?

Ⓐ Please
Ⓑ You please
● Would you please
Ⓓ You would please

10. _____ be happy to.

Ⓐ I
Ⓑ I'll
Ⓒ You
Ⓓ You'll

11. Could I possibly _____ a screwdriver?

Ⓐ borrow
Ⓑ borrow you
Ⓒ lend
Ⓓ lend me

12. _____ Here you are.

Ⓐ No.
Ⓑ I'll be happy to.
Ⓒ You'll be happy to.
Ⓓ Sure.

13. Thank you _____ your cell phone.

Ⓐ for borrowing
Ⓑ for lending you
Ⓒ for lending me
Ⓓ please lend me

14. _____ welcome.

Ⓐ You
Ⓑ Your
Ⓒ You're
Ⓓ I'm

15. _____ was your weekend?

Ⓐ Who
Ⓑ What
Ⓒ Where
Ⓓ How

16. _____ was great.

Ⓐ I
Ⓑ It
Ⓒ You
Ⓓ We

17. What _____?

Ⓐ you do
Ⓑ did you
Ⓒ you did
Ⓓ did you do

18. We _____ to the beach.

Ⓐ went
Ⓑ go
Ⓒ going
Ⓓ gone

10 Ⓐ Ⓑ Ⓒ Ⓓ
11 Ⓐ Ⓑ Ⓒ Ⓓ
12 Ⓐ Ⓑ Ⓒ Ⓓ
13 Ⓐ Ⓑ Ⓒ Ⓓ
14 Ⓐ Ⓑ Ⓒ Ⓓ
15 Ⓐ Ⓑ Ⓒ Ⓓ
16 Ⓐ Ⓑ Ⓒ Ⓓ
17 Ⓐ Ⓑ Ⓒ Ⓓ
18 Ⓐ Ⓑ Ⓒ Ⓓ

Go to the next page

Name ______________________________ Date ______________

C READING: Workplace Notes & Messages

Look at the notes and messages. Then do Numbers 19 through 22.

BizNet

Mr. Lu,

I'm sorry I was late this morning. My children's school bus didn't come this morning so I had to drive them to school. I'm writing my monthly report and will give it to you by the end of the day.

Thanks,
Gary

From the desk of
Wanda Torres

Alice,

Thank you for buying the pizza and soda for yesterday's office party. Everything was great, and all the employees enjoyed themselves. Please give me your receipts as soon as you can and I'll reimburse you.

Wanda

From: Dawn_Kendall@BizNet.com
To: Berta_Molina@BizNet.com
Subject: New employee

Berta,
Our new office assistant, Luis Rodriguez, will begin work next Monday. Unfortunately, I won't be here that day because I have some meetings out of town. Could you please show Luis around the office and introduce him to all the employees? Also, please show him how to use the telephone system and bring him to the personnel office so he can get the new employee manual and fill out a W-4 form. Luis can spend the rest of the day reading last year's company report. I'll meet with him on Tuesday morning and talk with him about his job responsibilities.
Thanks very much,
Dawn

19. Next Monday, Luis Rodriguez WON'T ____.

- Ⓐ fill out a W-4 form
- Ⓑ meet his co-workers
- Ⓒ meet with Dawn Kendall
- Ⓓ begin work at the company

20. An employee is apologizing for something in ____ of these notes and messages.

- Ⓐ three
- Ⓑ two
- Ⓒ one
- Ⓓ none

21. In the note from Wanda to Alice, *reimburse* means ____.

- Ⓐ Alice will give Wanda money
- Ⓑ Wanda will give Alice money
- Ⓒ Alice's salary will be higher
- Ⓓ Wanda will buy the pizza and soda next time

22. We can infer from these notes and messages that ____.

- Ⓐ Alice is Wanda's supervisor
- Ⓑ Luis is Berta's new supervisor
- Ⓒ Luis is Dawn's new supervisor
- Ⓓ Mr. Lu is Gary's supervisor

19 Ⓐ Ⓑ Ⓒ Ⓓ 20 Ⓐ Ⓑ Ⓒ Ⓓ 21 Ⓐ Ⓑ Ⓒ Ⓓ 22 Ⓐ Ⓑ Ⓒ Ⓓ

Go to the next page

D READING: A Paycheck & Pay Stub

Look at the paycheck and pay stub. Then do Numbers 23 through 28.

TECHNOFILE CORPORATION HADDAD F. EMP. NO. 46803
PAY PERIOD **PAY DATE:**
04/30/09 – 05/06/09 05/11/09

EARNINGS	RATE	HOURS	THIS PERIOD	YEAR TO DATE
REGULAR	16.00	35	560.00	7,280.00
OVERTIME	24.00	3	72.00	2,232.00
HOLIDAY	32.00	0	0.00	672.00
GROSS PAY			632.00	10,184.00
	THIS PERIOD	**YEAR TO DATE**	**GROSS PAY**	632.00
FED TAX	94.80	1,527.60	TAXES	170.64
FICA/MEDICARE	44.24	712.88	OTHER DEDUCTIONS	40.25
STATE TAX	31.60	509.20		
HEALTH	40.25	523.25		
			NET PAY	421.11

TECHNOFILE CORPORATION

Check No. 2689412

Date Issued 05/11/09

Pay to FAISAL HADDAD

FOUR HUNDRED TWENTY-ONE DOLLARS AND ELEVEN CENTS ***$421.11

Anna Rosario

23. Faisal's regular pay is _____.

Ⓐ $16.00 an hour
Ⓑ $24.00 an hour
Ⓒ $32.00 an hour
Ⓓ $35.00 an hour

24. He worked a total of _____ during this pay period.

Ⓐ 16 hours
Ⓑ 24 hours
Ⓒ 35 hours
Ⓓ 38 hours

25. A pay period at the Technofile Corporation is _____.

Ⓐ a day
Ⓑ a week
Ⓒ a month
Ⓓ a year

26. Faisal earned _____ during this pay period before taxes and other deductions.

Ⓐ $72.00
Ⓑ $560.00
Ⓒ $632.00
Ⓓ $10,184.00

27. The deduction for state taxes since the beginning of the year is _____.

Ⓐ $31.60
Ⓑ $94.80
Ⓒ $170.64
Ⓓ $509.20

28. The company deducted a total of _____ from Faisal's salary during this pay period.

Ⓐ $40.25
Ⓑ $170.64
Ⓒ $210.89
Ⓓ $421.11

23 Ⓐ Ⓑ Ⓒ Ⓓ 25 Ⓐ Ⓑ Ⓒ Ⓓ 27 Ⓐ Ⓑ Ⓒ Ⓓ

24 Ⓐ Ⓑ Ⓒ Ⓓ 26 Ⓐ Ⓑ Ⓒ Ⓓ 28 Ⓐ Ⓑ Ⓒ Ⓓ

Go to the next page

Name ______________________ Date __________

E CLOZE READING: Small Talk at Work

Choose the correct answers to complete the paragraph.

"Small talk" at work is important. The short conversations that people have with [its (A) / their (B) / our (C)] co-workers show that they [be (A) / was (B) / are (C)] 29 friendly. There are many good questions to begin small talk: "What [do (A) / did (B) / will (C)] 30 you do last weekend?" "What are you [will (A) / going (B) / going to (C)] 31 do next weekend?" "Did you see the football game on TV [yesterday (A) / tomorrow (B) / next week (C)] 32?" Other safe topics are hobbies, movies, TV programs, and the [weather (A) / weathers (B) / whether (C)] 33. You can talk about the news, but avoid [to talk (A) / talking (B) / don't talk (C)] 34 about politics. [Sharing (A) / Share (B) / You Share (C)] 35 information about your family can be a good topic for small talk, but co-workers won't like [hear (A) / listen (B) / hearing (C)] 36 about serious family problems. Listening is also an important part of small talk. [Listening (A) / Listen (B) / You listen (C)] 37 carefully to what your co-workers are saying, and ask questions to show you're interested.

F LISTENING ASSESSMENT: Two Co-Workers Talking at the Office

Read and listen to the questions. Then listen to the conversation and answer the questions.

38. Who just had a baby?
- (A) Tonya.
- (B) Leona.
- (C) Ken's wife.
- (D) Ken's sister.

39. What are Tonya and Barry thinking about doing?
- (A) Buying a house.
- (B) Getting an apartment outside the city.
- (C) Moving to a new apartment in their building.
- (D) Buying a new TV.

40. How did Ken go to Tampa?
- (A) He went by bus.
- (B) He probably went by airplane.
- (C) He went by car.
- (D) This information isn't in the conversation.

29 (A) (B) (C) (D)	33 (A) (B) (C) (D)	37 (A) (B) (C) (D)
30 (A) (B) (C) (D)	34 (A) (B) (C) (D)	38 (A) (B) (C) (D)
31 (A) (B) (C) (D)	35 (A) (B) (C) (D)	39 (A) (B) (C) (D)
32 (A) (B) (C) (D)	36 (A) (B) (C) (D)	40 (A) (B) (C) (D)

Go to the next page

G WRITING ASSESSMENT: A W-4 Form

Complete the form with your own information or make up any information you wish.

Form W-4

Purpose. Complete Form W-4 so that your employer can withhold the correct federal income tax from your pay.

Head of household. You are the head of household if you pay more than 50% of the costs of keeping up a home for yourself and your dependents.

Personal Allowances Worksheet

A Enter "1" for **yourself** if no one else can claim you as a dependent. .... A ______

B Enter "1" if
- You are single and have only one job; or
- You are married, have only one job, and your spouse does not work; or
- Your wages from a second job or your spouse's wages are $1,500 or less.

.... B ______

C Enter "1" for your **spouse**. .... C ______

D Enter number of **dependents**. .... D ______

E Enter "1" if you will file as **head of household** on your tax return. .... E ______

F Enter "1" if you have at least $1,500 of **child or dependent care expenses**. .... F ______

G **Child Tax Credit**
- If your total income is less than $58,000 ($86,000 if married), enter "2" for each child.
- If your total income is between $58,000 and $84,000 ($86,000 and $119,000 if married), enter "1" for each child. .... G ______

H Add lines A through G and enter total here. .... ▶ H ______

Stop here and enter the number from line H on line 5 of Form W-4 below.

Form **W-4** **Employee's Withholding Allowance Certificate**

1 Type or print your first name and middle initial.	Last name	**2** Your social security number
Home address (number and street or rural route)	**3** ☐ Single ☐ Married ☐ Married, but withhold at higher Single rate.	
City or town, state, and ZIP code	**4** If your last name is different from the one on your social security card, check here. You must call 1-800-772-1213 for a replacement card. ☐	
5 Total number of allowances you are claiming (from line **H** above)	**5**	
6 Additional amount, if any, you want withheld from each paycheck	**6**	
7 I claim exemption from withholding, and I meet **both** of the following conditions. ● Last year I had a right to a refund of **all** federal income tax withheld because I had **no** tax liability **and** ● This year I expect a refund of **all** federal income tax withheld because I expect to have **no** tax liability. If you meet both conditions write "Exempt" here ▶	**7**	
Under penalties of perjury, I declare that I have examined this certificate and to the best of my knowledge and belief, it is true, correct, and complete. **Employee's signature** (Form is not valid unless you sign it.) ▶	**Date** ▶	

H SPEAKING ASSESSMENT

I can ask and answer these questions:

Ask Answer

☐ ☐ What did you do last weekend?

☐ ☐ What are you going to do next weekend?

Ask Answer

☐ ☐ What do you enjoy doing in your free time?

☐ ☐ What do you avoid doing whenever you can?

STOP

Name ______________________________

Date ______________ Class ______________

8

A HEALTH & NUTRITION

Example:

I'd like to make ____.

- (A) cancel
- (B) reschedule
- (●) an appointment
- (D) a doctor's office

1. Can you ____ on Friday at 10:00?
   - (A) convenient
   - (B) convenient time
   - (C) come in
   - (D) would be fine

2. You should have a physical ____ every year.
   - (A) history
   - (B) examination
   - (C) vaccination
   - (D) prescription

3. I have to get a ____ shot.
   - (A) dental
   - (B) clinic
   - (C) cholesterol
   - (D) flu

4. Do you take any prescription ____?
   - (A) drugs
   - (B) operations
   - (C) tests
   - (D) diseases

5. The ____ on the food pyramid show the different food groups.
   - (A) grains
   - (B) products
   - (C) steps
   - (D) stripes

6. Dark green and orange vegetables contain more ____ than starchy vegetables.
   - (A) juice
   - (B) dairy products
   - (C) nutrients
   - (D) cholesterol

7. The oil from ____ is good for your heart.
   - (A) fish
   - (B) butter
   - (C) margarine
   - (D) ice cream

8. The grain group consists of foods made from wheat, rice, or ____.
   - (A) vegetables
   - (B) oils
   - (C) corn
   - (D) milk

9. I have a bad cough. I'm going to ____.
   - (A) go to the emergency room
   - (B) go to the clinic
   - (C) call 911
   - (D) get a vaccination

1 (A) (B) (C) (D) 4 (A) (B) (C) (D) 7 (A) (B) (C) (D)

2 (A) (B) (C) (D) 5 (A) (B) (C) (D) 8 (A) (B) (C) (D)

3 (A) (B) (C) (D) 6 (A) (B) (C) (D) 9 (A) (B) (C) (D)

Go to the next page

B GRAMMAR IN CONTEXT: Common Medical & Dental Problems

Example:
How long ____ coughing like this?
Ⓐ are you
Ⓑ you are
Ⓒ you've been
● have you been

10. ____ a few days.
Ⓐ Since
Ⓑ From
Ⓒ With
Ⓓ For

11. How long have your legs ____ swollen?
Ⓐ are
Ⓑ being
Ⓒ been
Ⓓ be

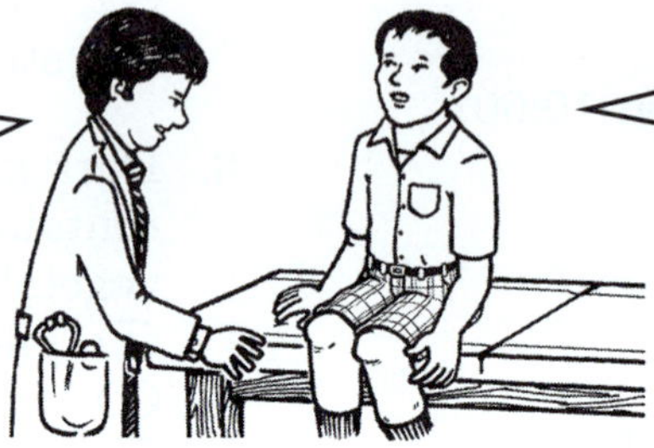

12. ____ last Monday.
Ⓐ Since
Ⓑ During
Ⓒ For
Ⓓ Began

13. When ____ first see these bruises on your arm?
Ⓐ you did
Ⓑ did you
Ⓒ you have
Ⓓ have you

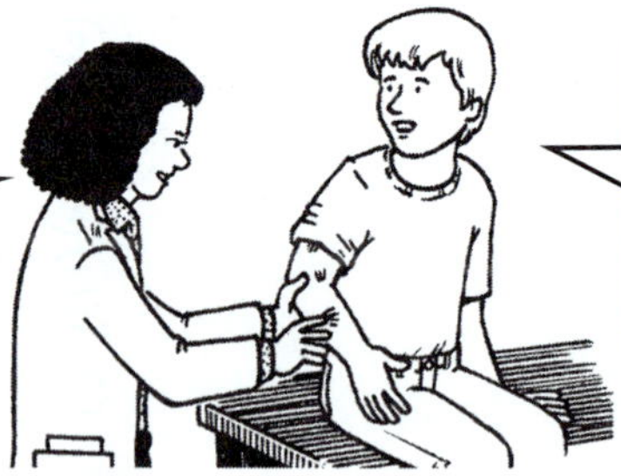

14. I don't know. ____ them for a while.
Ⓐ I'll have
Ⓑ I'm having
Ⓒ I had
Ⓓ I've had

15. ____ this area here feel tender?
Ⓐ Do
Ⓑ Does
Ⓒ Have
Ⓓ Has

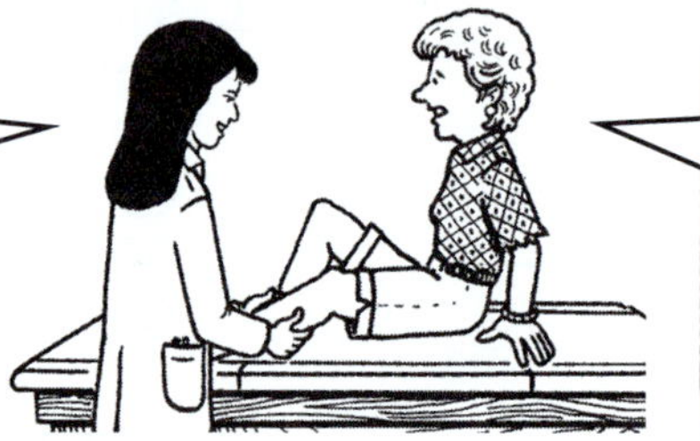

16. Ouch! Yes. ____ felt tender since I fell down the stairs.
Ⓐ I
Ⓑ They have
Ⓒ It has
Ⓓ I was

17. You have a ____. I can take care of it today.
Ⓐ filling
Ⓑ tooth
Ⓒ gum
Ⓓ cavity

18. Can I have a silver ____?
Ⓐ filling
Ⓑ tooth
Ⓒ gum
Ⓓ cavity

Yes, you can.

Okay.

10 Ⓐ Ⓑ Ⓒ Ⓓ
11 Ⓐ Ⓑ Ⓒ Ⓓ
12 Ⓐ Ⓑ Ⓒ Ⓓ
13 Ⓐ Ⓑ Ⓒ Ⓓ
14 Ⓐ Ⓑ Ⓒ Ⓓ
15 Ⓐ Ⓑ Ⓒ Ⓓ
16 Ⓐ Ⓑ Ⓒ Ⓓ
17 Ⓐ Ⓑ Ⓒ Ⓓ
18 Ⓐ Ⓑ Ⓒ Ⓓ

Go to the next page

Name ____________________ Date ____________

C READING: Medical Appointment Cards

These people have medical appointments during the next few months. Read the appointment cards. Then do Numbers 19 through 22.

COMMUNITY MEDICAL CLINIC
4600 N. Federal Highway, Miami, FL 33137

Quan Vu
HAS AN APPOINTMENT ON
Mon. (DAY) Oct. (MONTH) 10th (DATE) at 11 A.M. (circled) P.M.

IF UNABLE TO KEEP THIS APPOINTMENT, PLEASE GIVE ONE DAY ADVANCE NOTICE.
TELEPHONE: (305) 576-7000

APPOINTMENT

FOR Gloria Salinas
ON Thu. (DAY) Nov. (MONTH) 3 (DATE) AT 2:00 A.M. P.M. (circled)

GLENDALE HEALTH CENTER
501 North Glendale Avenue
Glendale, CA 91206
(818) 500-8762

IF UNABLE TO KEEP THIS APPOINTMENT, KINDLY GIVE 24 HOURS NOTICE.

M Ahmed Samra
HAS AN APPOINTMENT ON
☐ MON ☐ TUE ☐ WED ☐ THU ☐ FRI ☑ SAT
OCT (MONTH) 22 (DATE) AT 3:15 A.M. P.M. (circled)

SUNNYSIDE HEALTH CENTER
9314 Cullen Blvd. TEL (713) 732-5000
Houston, TX 77051

PATIENTS WILL BE CHARGED FOR APPOINTMENTS NOT CANCELED AT LEAST 24 HOURS IN ADVANCE.

KOMED HOLMAN HEALTH CENTER
4259 S. Berkelely Street
Chicago, Illinois 60653
TEL 773.268.7600

Jane Harper
HAS AN APPOINTMENT ON
Tue. (DAY) Jan. (MONTH) 3 (DATE) AT 1:30 A.M. P.M. (circled)

IF APPOINTMENT CANNOT BE KEPT, NOTIFICATION SHOULD BE MADE ONE DAY IN ADVANCE.

19. Which day of the week is Gloria's appointment?
- (A) Tuesday
- (B) Thursday
- (C) November
- (D) the 3rd

20. Which patient has an appointment in the morning?
- (A) Jane Harper
- (B) Gloria Salinas
- (C) Ahmed Samra
- (D) Quan Vu

21. Which health center is definitely open during part of the weekend?
- (A) Community Medical Clinic
- (B) Glendale Health Center
- (C) Sunnyside Health Center
- (D) Komed Holman Health Center

22. Whose appointment is next year?
- (A) Jane Harper
- (B) Gloria Salinas
- (C) Ahmed Samra
- (D) Quan Vu

19 (A) (B) (C) (D) 20 (A) (B) (C) (D) 21 (A) (B) (C) (D) 22 (A) (B) (C) (D)

Go to the next page

D MAJOR INTERNAL ORGANS

Look at the illustrations. Choose the correct answer.

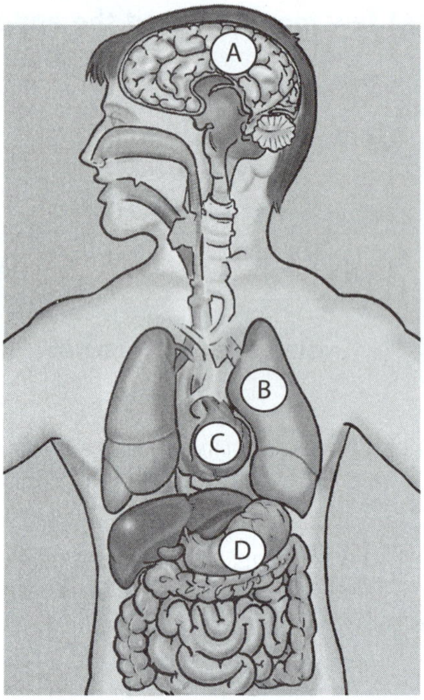

Example: stomach Ⓐ Ⓑ Ⓒ ●

23. brain Ⓐ Ⓑ Ⓒ Ⓓ

24. heart Ⓐ Ⓑ Ⓒ Ⓓ

25. lungs Ⓐ Ⓑ Ⓒ Ⓓ

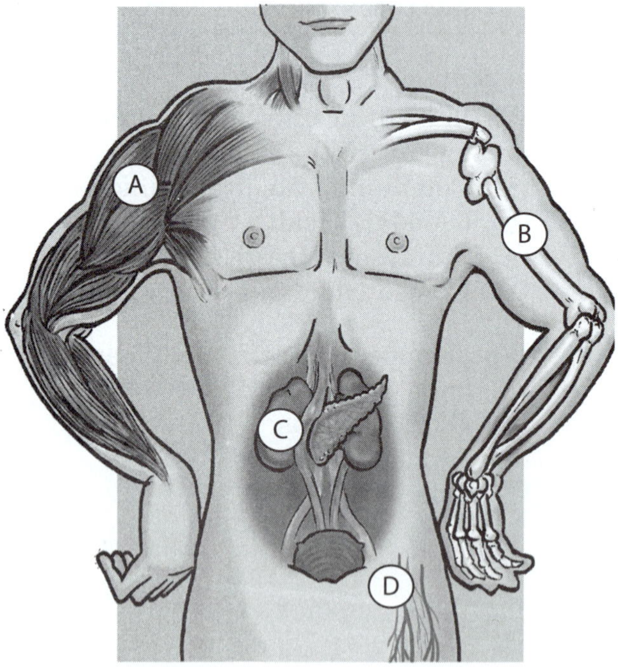

26. veins Ⓐ Ⓑ Ⓒ Ⓓ

27. bones Ⓐ Ⓑ Ⓒ Ⓓ

28. kidneys Ⓐ Ⓑ Ⓒ Ⓓ

29. muscles Ⓐ Ⓑ Ⓒ Ⓓ

23 Ⓐ Ⓑ Ⓒ Ⓓ 25 Ⓐ Ⓑ Ⓒ Ⓓ 27 Ⓐ Ⓑ Ⓒ Ⓓ 29 Ⓐ Ⓑ Ⓒ Ⓓ
24 Ⓐ Ⓑ Ⓒ Ⓓ 26 Ⓐ Ⓑ Ⓒ Ⓓ 28 Ⓐ Ⓑ Ⓒ Ⓓ

Go to the next page

Name ______________________________ Date ______________

E CLOZE READING: Public Health Information

Choose the correct answers to complete the newspaper article.

New Health Center Opens

WARNER—The new Downtown Health Center opened yesterday. The [examination (A) / clinic (B, filled) / emergency (C)] offers health care to all city residents. It is a drop-in medical center, so no [service (A) / routine (B) / appointment (C)] 30 is necessary. For patients who don't understand English well, [vaccination (A) / translation (B) / medication (C)] 31 is available in 15 different languages. Patients pay for medical care based on how much they earn since the clinic's fees are on a sliding [scale (A) / range (B) / care (C)] 32. Patients can have a physical [guideline (A) / operation (B) / examination (C)] 33 every year, including a [cholesterol (A) / tetanus (B) / skin (C)] 34 blood test and other screening tests. The clinic also provides flu shots and other [prescriptions (A) / vaccinations (B) / schedules (C)] 35. It is across the street from Warner General Hospital, a full-service hospital with 500 beds and a 24-hour [serious (A) / 911 (B) / emergency (C)] 36 room. Patients should go there or call an ambulance for health problems such as [a cough (A) / a broken leg (B) / an earache (C)] 37.

Patients with routine medical problems should use the clinic.

F LISTENING ASSESSMENT: Calling about a Medical Appointment

Read and listen to the questions. Then listen to the conversation and answer the questions.

38. Why is Victoria calling the doctor's office?

- (A) To make a new appointment.
- (B) To cancel an appointment.
- (C) To reschedule an appointment.
- (D) To confirm an appointment.

39. When was she scheduled to come in?

- (A) Thu. Apr. 15 4:00
- (B) Tue. Apr. 20 11:00
- (C) Thu. Apr. 20 11:00
- (D) Tue. Apr. 13 10:00

40. When is her new appointment?

- (A) Thu. Apr. 15 4:00
- (B) Tue. Apr. 20 11:00
- (C) Thu. Apr. 20 11:00
- (D) Tue. Apr. 13 10:00

30 (A) (B) (C) (D)
31 (A) (B) (C) (D)
32 (A) (B) (C) (D)
33 (A) (B) (C) (D)
34 (A) (B) (C) (D)
35 (A) (B) (C) (D)
36 (A) (B) (C) (D)
37 (A) (B) (C) (D)
38 (A) (B) (C) (D)
39 (A) (B) (C) (D)
40 (A) (B) (C) (D)

Go to the next page

G WRITING ASSESSMENT: A Medical History Form

Complete the form with your own information or make up any information you wish.

MEDICAL HISTORY

Name ______________________ **Date of Birth** ______________

List the medications you are now taking. Include non-prescription drugs and vitamins.

____

List any allergies you have to drugs, food, or other items. ______________

____

List any operations you have had, including the year. ______________

____

Please check if you have had any of the following health problems.

____ chicken pox	____ diabetes	____ depression
____ measles	____ tuberculosis	____ frequent earaches
____ mumps	____ cancer	____ severe headaches
____ asthma	____ AIDS	____ back problems
____ heart disease	____ kidney disease	____ frequent colds
____ high blood pressure	____ liver disease (hepatitis)	____ stomach problems
____ pneumonia	____ influenza	____ loss of appetite

FAMILY HISTORY

Please check if anyone in your family (parents, siblings, grandparents, children) has had any of the following illnesses.

____ asthma	____ diabetes	____ AIDS
____ heart disease	____ tuberculosis	____ kidney disease
____ high blood pressure	____ cancer	____ liver disease

RECORD OF IMMUNIZATIONS

Please check if you had any of the following vaccinations or tests, and fill in the year of the most recent ones.

	Year
____ measles	
____ mumps	
____ chicken pox	
____ tetanus	

	Year
____ tuberculosis test	
____ hepatitis B	
____ influenza	
____ pneumonia	

H SPEAKING ASSESSMENT

I can ask and answer these questions:

Ask	Answer	
☐	☐	How often do you have a physical examination at a doctor's office or a clinic?
☐	☐	Where do you go for medical care?
☐	☐	What vegetables and fruit do you eat?
☐	☐	What foods should you eat more of?
☐	☐	What foods should you eat less of?

STOP

Name ______________________________

Date ______________ Class ______________

9

A SHOPPING

Example:

I'm _____ a pair of pants.
- (A) want
- (B) need
- (C) looking
- ● looking for

1. This dress is 20% off this week. We're having a special _____.
   - (A) regular price
   - (B) half-price
   - (C) sale
   - (D) reduced

2. You can try on these pants in the _____.
   - (A) mall
   - (B) cleaner's
   - (C) pants room
   - (D) dressing room

3. I like to buy things when they're _____.
   - (A) discount
   - (B) on sale
   - (C) the sign on the rack
   - (D) bargain

4. My jacket size is _____.
   - (A) 20% off
   - (B) half-price
   - (C) large
   - (D) reduced

5. I don't want to exchange it. I'd like _____, please.
   - (A) the matter
   - (B) a return
   - (C) a receipt
   - (D) a refund

6. All our shirts are 15 _____ off the regular price this week.
   - (A) percent
   - (B) price
   - (C) reduced
   - (D) half

7. You can use this coupon until the _____.
   - (A) regular price
   - (B) expiration date
   - (C) newspaper ad
   - (D) refund

8. These tee shirts are usually $16, but they're only $12 this week. They're _____.
   - (A) 10% off
   - (B) 20% off
   - (C) 25% off
   - (D) half-price

9. All our $60 men's jeans are $40 this week. They're _____ the regular price.
   - (A) 1/3 off
   - (B) 1/2 off
   - (C) 20% off
   - (D) 40% off

1 (A) (B) (C) (D)	4 (A) (B) (C) (D)	7 (A) (B) (C) (D)
2 (A) (B) (C) (D)	5 (A) (B) (C) (D)	8 (A) (B) (C) (D)
3 (A) (B) (C) (D)	6 (A) (B) (C) (D)	9 (A) (B) (C) (D)

Go to the next page

B GRAMMAR IN CONTEXT: Exchanging & Returning Defective Products

Example:
I'd like to exchange _____ jacket.
● this
(B) that
(C) these
(D) those

10. What's the matter with _____?
(A) you
(B) that
(C) this
(D) it

11. Three buttons _____ missing.
(A) be
(B) is
(C) are
(D) will be

12. All right. Please get another jacket from the rack, _____ here, and I'll be happy to help you.
(A) bring back
(B) bring it back
(C) bring back it
(D) it bring back

13. I'd like to return _____ pants.
(A) this
(B) that
(C) these
(D) those

14. What's the matter with _____?
(A) it
(B) you
(C) those
(D) them

15. The zipper _____ broken.
(A) be
(B) is
(C) are
(D) did

16. _____ your receipt?
(A) You have
(B) Do have
(C) Do you have
(D) You do have

17. Yes. _____
(A) Here it is.
(B) Here I am.
(C) Here they are.
(D) It is.

18. _____ exchange them?
(A) Do you like to
(B) You do like to
(C) You would like to
(D) Would you like to

19. No, thank you. _____ a refund, please.
(A) I like
(B) I'd like
(C) I'll like
(D) You give

20. Okay. Here's our merchandise return form. Please _____ and I'll give you a refund.
(A) fill
(B) fill out
(C) fill out it
(D) fill it out

10 (A) (B) (C) (D)
11 (A) (B) (C) (D)
12 (A) (B) (C) (D)
13 (A) (B) (C) (D)
14 (A) (B) (C) (D)
15 (A) (B) (C) (D)
16 (A) (B) (C) (D)
17 (A) (B) (C) (D)
18 (A) (B) (C) (D)
19 (A) (B) (C) (D)
20 (A) (B) (C) (D)

Go to the next page

Name ______________________ Date ______________

C READING: A Store Advertisement

Look at the clothing store advertisement. Then do Numbers 21 through 24.

21. During the sale, Speedway Running Shoes are _____.

- Ⓐ 10% off
- Ⓑ 40% off
- Ⓒ $80.00
- Ⓓ half-price

22. Fatima is going to buy four tee shirts during the sale. How much is she going to spend?

- Ⓐ $50
- Ⓑ $60
- Ⓒ $70
- Ⓓ $80

23. The regular price of Nina Sanders skirts is _____.

- Ⓐ $25
- Ⓑ $50
- Ⓒ $75
- Ⓓ $100

24. The men's jeans are _____ during the sale.

- Ⓐ 10% off
- Ⓑ 20% off
- Ⓒ 25% off
- Ⓓ 30% off

21 Ⓐ Ⓑ Ⓒ Ⓓ 22 Ⓐ Ⓑ Ⓒ Ⓓ 23 Ⓐ Ⓑ Ⓒ Ⓓ 24 Ⓐ Ⓑ Ⓒ Ⓓ

Go to the next page

D READING: Store Coupons

Look at the coupons for these food products. Then do Numbers 25 through 30.

25. You bought a loaf of Alan's bread with a coupon and paid $2.00. The original price was _____.

- Ⓐ $1.50
- Ⓑ $2.00
- Ⓒ $2.50
- Ⓓ $3.00

26. A box of Happy Heart cereal costs $3.00. With a coupon you pay _____ for three boxes.

- Ⓐ $5.00
- Ⓑ $6.00
- Ⓒ $7.50
- Ⓓ $9.00

27. You can't use the coupon for _____ after September 18, 2012.

- Ⓐ Bob & Joe's Ice Cream
- Ⓑ Maxima Coffee
- Ⓒ Farmtown Yogurt
- Ⓓ Pollyana Jam

28. Ramona bought one pint of Bob & Joe's Ice Cream. The regular price is $4.50. She paid _____.

- Ⓐ $1.00
- Ⓑ $3.50
- Ⓒ $4.00
- Ⓓ $4.50

29. A 6 oz. container of Farmtown Yogurt costs $1.00. With a coupon you pay a total of _____ when you buy ten.

- Ⓐ $9.00
- Ⓑ $9.50
- Ⓒ $10.00
- Ⓓ 90¢

30. You bought two cans of Maxima Coffee with a coupon and paid $9.00. The regular price of one can is _____.

- Ⓐ $4.50
- Ⓑ $5.00
- Ⓒ $5.50
- Ⓓ $6.00

25 Ⓐ Ⓑ Ⓒ Ⓓ 27 Ⓐ Ⓑ Ⓒ Ⓓ 29 Ⓐ Ⓑ Ⓒ Ⓓ

26 Ⓐ Ⓑ Ⓒ Ⓓ 28 Ⓐ Ⓑ Ⓒ Ⓓ 30 Ⓐ Ⓑ Ⓒ Ⓓ

Go to the next page

Name ______________________________ Date ______________

E CLOZE READING: A Store Return Policy

Choose the correct answers to complete the sign in a store's Customer Service Department.

Pratt's Department Store

Our Return Policy

- You may receipt (A) refund (B) return (●) most items within 90 days of the date of purchase.
- We will back (A) take back (B) take them back (C) [31] computers and printers only within 45 days of the date of purchase.
- If you want to return CDs or DVDs, you must bring (A) bring back (B) bring them back (C) [32] within 30 days of the date of purchase, and they must be opened (A) unopened (B) on sale (C) [33].
- We cannot accept returns on items marked Final Sale (A) Refund (B) Credit (C) [34].
- To receive a refund, you must provide your return (A) receipt (B) purchase (C) [35] for the item. If you don't have it, you can buy (A) accept (B) exchange (C) [36] the item for another one or you can receive a gift card with a store credit for the amount of the purchase.
- You may return a defective item at any time, and we will repair (A) break (B) buy (C) [37] it or give you a new item.

F LISTENING ASSESSMENT: Returning Items to a Store

Read and listen to the questions. Then listen to the conversation and answer the questions.

38. How many items is the customer returning to the store?

- (A) One.
- (B) Two.
- (C) Three.
- (D) Four.

39. What's the matter with the blouse?

- (A) A button is missing.
- (B) Two buttons are missing.
- (C) A sleeve is stained.
- (D) The sleeves are stained.

40. Why can't the customer receive a refund?

- (A) The coat and the blouse are defective.
- (B) The customer wants to exchange the items.
- (C) The customer doesn't have a gift card.
- (D) The customer doesn't have the receipt.

31 (A) (B) (C) (D)	34 (A) (B) (C) (D)	37 (A) (B) (C) (D)	40 (A) (B) (C) (D)
32 (A) (B) (C) (D)	35 (A) (B) (C) (D)	38 (A) (B) (C) (D)	
33 (A) (B) (C) (D)	36 (A) (B) (C) (D)	39 (A) (B) (C) (D)	

Go to the next page

G WRITING ASSESSMENT: A Product Return Form

You are returning an item to a store in your community. Complete the form with your personal information, and make up information about the product you are returning.

PRODUCT RETURN FORM

1. CUSTOMER INFORMATION

Name ______________________________

Address ______________________________

City ____________________ State _____ Zip Code __________

Telephone: Home (______) ______- __________ Work (______) ______- __________

2. PRODUCT INFORMATION

Product being returned: ______________________________

Store where purchased (name, city, state): ______________________________

Purchase date: ______________________________

Please describe problem with product: ______________________________

____

3. REFUND/EXCHANGE INFORMATION

Please check one:

_____ I request a refund. (Store receipt required.)

_____ I will exchange the product for another one of the same item.

_____ I request a store credit for the amount of the purchase.

_____ Other (Explain: ______________________________)

Customer Signature: ______________________________ Today's Date: __________

H SPEAKING ASSESSMENT

I can ask and answer these questions:

Ask	Answer	
☐	☐	Where do you shop for clothing?
☐	☐	What kind of clothing do you like to wear?
☐	☐	Have you ever bought something on sale?
☐	☐	What did you buy, and where?
☐	☐	Have you ever returned an item to a store?
☐	☐	What did you return, and where?

STOP

Name ______________________________

Date ______________ Class ______________

10

A WORKPLACE COMMUNICATION & CAREER ADVANCEMENT

Example:

Excuse me. Can you ____?

- Ⓐ I help
- Ⓑ my help
- ● help me
- Ⓓ me help

1. Please ____ make a copy.
   - Ⓐ how to
   - Ⓑ show me how
   - Ⓒ you show me how to
   - Ⓓ show me how to

2. ____, add the water. Then, press the ON button.
   - Ⓐ Sure
   - Ⓑ First
   - Ⓒ Finally
   - Ⓓ And finally

3. I'm friendly at work. I ____ my co-workers.
   - Ⓐ get
   - Ⓑ get along
   - Ⓒ get along with
   - Ⓓ along with

4. I try to always have a positive ____ at work.
   - Ⓐ compliment
   - Ⓑ attitude
   - Ⓒ feedback
   - Ⓓ promotion

5. Appropriate clothes and good grooming are important parts of your ____ at work.
   - Ⓐ appearance
   - Ⓑ opportunity
   - Ⓒ energy
   - Ⓓ creativity

6. When a co-worker does something well, ____.
   - Ⓐ apologize
   - Ⓑ complain
   - Ⓒ volunteer
   - Ⓓ give a compliment

7. It's important to continue your ____ to learn new skills.
   - Ⓐ promotion
   - Ⓑ evaluation
   - Ⓒ education
   - Ⓓ presentation

8. If you want to move ahead at work, ask for more ____.
   - Ⓐ skills
   - Ⓑ responsibilities
   - Ⓒ compliments
   - Ⓓ grades

9. I'm going to take a ____ course so that my memos, letters, and reports are better.
   - Ⓐ Customer Service
   - Ⓑ Bookkeeping
   - Ⓒ Public Speaking
   - Ⓓ Business Writing

1 Ⓐ Ⓑ Ⓒ Ⓓ	4 Ⓐ Ⓑ Ⓒ Ⓓ	7 Ⓐ Ⓑ Ⓒ Ⓓ
2 Ⓐ Ⓑ Ⓒ Ⓓ	5 Ⓐ Ⓑ Ⓒ Ⓓ	8 Ⓐ Ⓑ Ⓒ Ⓓ
3 Ⓐ Ⓑ Ⓒ Ⓓ	6 Ⓐ Ⓑ Ⓒ Ⓓ	9 Ⓐ Ⓑ Ⓒ Ⓓ

Go to the next page

B GRAMMAR IN CONTEXT: Giving & Following a Sequence of Instructions

Example:
Excuse me, Rosa. _____ help me?
Ⓐ I can
Ⓑ You can
Ⓒ Can I
● Can you

10. Sure. _____ help?
Ⓐ How I can
Ⓑ How you can
Ⓒ How can I
Ⓓ How can you

11. _____ how to turn on the alarm system?
Ⓐ You can show me
Ⓑ Can you show me
Ⓒ I can show you
Ⓓ Can I show you

12. Sure. _____
Ⓐ I'll be happy.
Ⓑ I'll be happy to.
Ⓒ You'll be happy.
Ⓓ You'll be happy to.

13. _____
Ⓐ I see.
Ⓑ That's correct.
Ⓒ You're welcome.
Ⓓ Thanks.

14. _____, close the door.
_____, enter the code.
Ⓐ Then . . . After that
Ⓑ Then . . . First
Ⓒ First . . . Then
Ⓓ Finally . . . Then

15. _____
Ⓐ I see.
Ⓑ You see.
Ⓒ Yes. That's correct.
Ⓓ Excuse me.

16. _____, press ON.
_____, leave the building.
Ⓐ First . . . Then
Ⓑ First . . . And finally
Ⓒ After that . . . First
Ⓓ After that . . . And finally

17. I press ON and leave the building. _____
Ⓐ Can you help me?
Ⓑ How can I help?
Ⓒ Is that right?
Ⓓ Are you right?

18. Yes. _____
Ⓐ I'm correct.
Ⓑ That's correct.
Ⓒ Thanks very much.
Ⓓ That isn't right.

10 Ⓐ Ⓑ Ⓒ Ⓓ	13 Ⓐ Ⓑ Ⓒ Ⓓ	16 Ⓐ Ⓑ Ⓒ Ⓓ
11 Ⓐ Ⓑ Ⓒ Ⓓ	14 Ⓐ Ⓑ Ⓒ Ⓓ	17 Ⓐ Ⓑ Ⓒ Ⓓ
12 Ⓐ Ⓑ Ⓒ Ⓓ	15 Ⓐ Ⓑ Ⓒ Ⓓ	18 Ⓐ Ⓑ Ⓒ Ⓓ

Go to the next page

Name ______________________ Date ____________

C READING: A Job Performance Evaluation

Look at this employee's job performance evaluation. Then do Numbers 19 through 22.

Employee Name Manuel Garcia   Position Stock clerk

	Excellent	Good	Needs Improvement	Unsatisfactory
The employee understands the job responsibilities.	✓			
The employee has the skills needed to do the job.		✓		
The employee communicates clearly.			✓	
The employee listens carefully to supervisors and co-workers.			✓	
The employee gets along well with co-workers.		✓		
The employee has a positive attitude.	✓			
The employee is dependable and hardworking.	✓			
The employee is polite and friendly with customers.				
The employee solves problems creatively.			✓	
The employee dresses appropriately.		✓		
The employee is well groomed.	✓			
The employee learns from feedback.			✓	
The employee continues to learn new skills.	✓			

Employee's Signature *Manuel Garcia*   Date of Evaluation 12/14/09

Evaluated by (Print) Larissa Silver   Evaluator's Signature *Larissa Silver*

19. The employee has ____ grades that are Excellent or Good.
- (A) three
- (B) five
- (C) eight
- (D) twelve

20. Larissa is Manuel Garcia's ____.
- (A) supervisor
- (B) stock clerk
- (C) employee
- (D) customer

21. We can infer that ____.
- (A) the employee doesn't like his job
- (B) the employee doesn't work hard
- (C) the employee doesn't have very good listening and speaking skills
- (D) the employee isn't dependable

22. One line of the evaluation form is not filled in. This is probably because ____.
- (A) the employee isn't friendly with customers
- (B) the employee isn't polite with customers
- (C) customers complain about the employee
- (D) the employee doesn't communicate with customers in his job

19 (A) (B) (C) (D)   20 (A) (B) (C) (D)   21 (A) (B) (C) (D)   22 (A) (B) (C) (D)

Go to the next page

D READING: A Course Catalog

Look at the adult education catalog. Then do Numbers 23 through 26.

ADULT EDUCATION COURSES—FALL TERM

BUSINESS

BUS 101 Business Procedures—M, W, F
Learn the procedures in a business office. Topics include filing, telephone skills, receiving and sending mail, organizing meetings and conferences, scheduling appointments, making travel reservations, and time management.

BUS 105 Business Writing—M, W
This course helps students learn to write clear and concise business letters, memos, and reports.

BUS 201 Bookkeeping—M, Tu, W, Th, F
This course prepares students for the national Certified Bookkeeper examination. Topics include payroll (paying wages, reporting taxes) and inventory.

BUS 205 Entrepreneurship—W, F
Learn how to start and operate your own business. Each student will develop a business plan.

COMPUTERS

COM 101 Microsoft Word I—Tu, Th
Students will learn to create documents with the popular word processing software.

COM 102 Microsoft Outlook—F
Learn to use Microsoft Outlook to send, receive, and organize electronic mail.

COM 106 Excel Spreadsheets—Tu, Th
Balancing a checkbook and calculating family expenses is easier with Excel software. This course covers the basics of spreadsheets.

COM 201 Microsoft Word II—W, Th, F
Use the advanced features of Word to create documents with charts. Students will also learn to create newsletters and flyers.

COM 203 PowerPoint Presentations—M, F
Learn to create professional-looking presentations that include graphs, charts, and pictures using PowerPoint.

CULINARY ARTS

CA 100 Food Preparation—M, Tu, W, Th, F
Students learn kitchen procedures and basic recipes for an entry-level position as a Food and Beverage Specialist in a hotel, hospital, or restaurant kitchen.

CA 104 Food Sanitation—W, F
Learn how to prepare food safely. This course teaches health regulations and procedures and the reasons for them.

HEALTH SCIENCE

HS 101 CPR (Cardiopulmonary Resuscitation)—M
This course covers emergency procedures to follow when someone has stopped breathing or the heart has stopped beating. Red Cross certification.

23. Microsoft Word is software for _____.

- (A) giving presentations
- (B) sending and receiving e-mail
- (C) making spreadsheets
- (D) writing documents

24. Sonia and Mercedes are planning to start their own cleaning service company. They're going to take the course in _____ to prepare to open their business.

- (A) Entrepreneurship
- (B) Business Writing
- (C) CPR
- (D) Food Preparation

25. Julio can only take adult education courses on Tuesdays and Thursdays because of his work schedule. He's thinking about taking Course Number _____.

- (A) BUS 105
- (B) HS 101
- (C) COM 106
- (D) CA 100

26. Course Number _____ prepares students to take a national examination.

- (A) BUS 101
- (B) BUS 201
- (C) COM 106
- (D) CA 100

23 (A) (B) (C) (D)   24 (A) (B) (C) (D)   25 (A) (B) (C) (D)   26 (A) (B) (C) (D)

Go to the next page

Name ______________________________ Date ______________

E CLOZE READING: A Promotion at Work

Choose the correct answers to complete the memo.

CREATIVE COMPUTER SOLUTIONS

Interoffice Memorandum

TO: All Employees
FROM: Jane Hamilton, Director
SUBJECT: Promotion of Karima Mansoor

I am happy to announce the [evaluation (A) / promotion (B, filled in) / education (C)] of Karima Mansoor to the position of office manager. You all know that Karima has been doing an excellent job as assistant manager. She's [hard work (A) / work hard (B) / hardworking (C)] 27 and enthusiastic. She [gets along (A) / knows (B) / takes care (C)] 28 well with everyone in the office, she [works (A) / communicates (B) / understands (C)] 29 clearly, and she thinks [around (A) / inside (B) / outside (C)] 30 the box to find new ways to solve problems. Karima has recently finished a [grooming (A) / training (B) / solving (C)] 31 program that has prepared her well for this new position. She has completed a year of coursework in [culinary (A) / sanitation (B) / business (C)] 32 procedures, and she has received the highest [grades (A) / reports (B) / notes (C)] 33 possible in this program. Karima's supervisor, Lidiya Sorreno, has given Karima excellent job [appearance (A) / performance (B) / opportunity (C)] 34 evaluations during the past three years. Now that Lidiya has been promoted to the [position (A) / attitude (B) / evaluation (C)] 35 of Director of Personnel, we have decided that Karima is the best person to take Lidiya's place. We know that Karima will do well with her new [supervisors (A) / responsibilities (B) / problems (C)] 36. She has worked hard for our company, and I know you agree that she [receives (A) / serves (B) / deserves (C)] 37 this promotion.

27 Ⓐ Ⓑ Ⓒ Ⓓ
28 Ⓐ Ⓑ Ⓒ Ⓓ
29 Ⓐ Ⓑ Ⓒ Ⓓ
30 Ⓐ Ⓑ Ⓒ Ⓓ
31 Ⓐ Ⓑ Ⓒ Ⓓ
32 Ⓐ Ⓑ Ⓒ Ⓓ
33 Ⓐ Ⓑ Ⓒ Ⓓ
34 Ⓐ Ⓑ Ⓒ Ⓓ
35 Ⓐ Ⓑ Ⓒ Ⓓ
36 Ⓐ Ⓑ Ⓒ Ⓓ
37 Ⓐ Ⓑ Ⓒ Ⓓ

Go to the next page

F LISTENING ASSESSMENT: Following a Sequence of Instructions

Read and listen to the questions. Then listen to the conversation and answer the questions.

38. When is the copy machine ready to print?
    - (A) When the paper is regular size.
    - (B) When the Start button is green.
    - (C) When the lid is up.
    - (D) When the green light is on.

39. What does the employee need to copy?
    - (A) One regular-size page.
    - (B) One large-size page.
    - (C) Fifty regular-size pages.
    - (D) Fifty large-size pages.

40. How can someone copy a large map on this machine?
    - (A) Put it face down in the automatic document feeder.
    - (B) Put it face up in the automatic document feeder.
    - (C) Put it face down on the glass.
    - (D) Put it face up on the glass.

G WRITING ASSESSMENT: Your Education History & Education Plan

Fill out the form. Write information about the schools you have attended, the skills you have, and your education plans for the future.

EDUCATION HISTORY

______ Dates	______ Degree or certificate
	______ School, City, State
______ Dates	______ Degree or certificate
	______ School, City, State
______ Dates	______ Degree or certificate
	______ School, City, State

SKILLS

______

EDUCATION PLANS FOR THE FUTURE

What you plan to study:	Where (Name or type of school):	When (Year):
______	______	______
______	______	______
______	______	______

H SPEAKING ASSESSMENT

I can ask and answer these questions:

Ask	Answer	
☐	☐	Tell me about your skills.
☐	☐	Tell me about your educational background.
☐	☐	What job do you want in the future?
☐	☐	What new skills do you want to learn in the future?

STOP

38 (A) (B) (C) (D) 39 (A) (B) (C) (D) 40 (A) (B) (C) (D)

APPENDIX

Listening Scripts

Page 7 Exercise H

Listen to each question and then complete the answer.

1. Does Jim like to play soccer?
2. Is Alice working today?
3. Are those students staying after school today?
4. Do Mr. and Mrs. Jackson work hard?
5. Does your wife still write poetry?
6. Is it raining?
7. Is he busy?
8. Do you have to leave?
9. Does your sister play the violin?
10. Is your brother studying in the library?
11. Are you wearing a necklace today?
12. Do you and your husband go camping very often?
13. Is your niece doing her homework?
14. Are they still chatting online?
15. Do you and your friends play Scrabble very often?

Page 13 Exercise B

Listen and circle the correct answer.

1. They work.
2. They worked.
3. We study English.
4. I waited for the bus.
5. We visit our friends.
6. She met important people.
7. He taught Chinese.
8. She delivers the mail.
9. I wrote letters to my friends.
10. I ride my bicycle to work.
11. He sleeps very well.
12. I had a terrible headache.

Page 26 Exercise C

Listen and choose the time of the action.

1. My daughter is going to sing Broadway show tunes in her high school show.
2. Janet bought a new dress for her friend's party.
3. Are you going to go out with George?
4. I went shopping at the new mall.
5. How did you poke yourself in the eye?
6. Who's going to prepare dinner?
7. Did the baby sleep well?
8. I'm really looking forward to Saturday night.
9. Is your son going to play games on his computer?
10. We're going to complain to the landlord about the heat in our apartment.
11. We bought a dozen donuts.
12. I'm going to take astronomy.

Page 33 Exercise L

Listen to each story. Then answer the questions.

What Are Mr. and Mrs. Miller Looking Forward to?

Mr. and Mrs. Miller moved into their new house in Los Angeles last week. They're happy because the house has a large, bright living room and a big, beautiful yard. They're looking forward to life in their new home. Every weekend they'll be able to relax in their living room and enjoy the beautiful California weather in their big, beautiful yard. But this weekend Mr. and Mrs. Miller won't be relaxing. They're going to be very busy. First, they're going to repaint the living room. Then, they're going to assemble their new computer and VCR. And finally, they're going to plant some flowers in their yard. They'll finally be able to relax NEXT weekend.

What's Jonathan Looking Forward to?

I'm so excited! I'm sitting at my computer in my office, but I'm not thinking about my work today. I'm thinking about next weekend because next Saturday is the day I'll be getting married. After the wedding, my wife and I will be going to Hawaii for a week. I can't wait! For one week, we won't be working, we won't be cooking, we won't be cleaning, and we won't be paying bills. We'll be swimming in the ocean, relaxing on the beach, and eating in fantastic restaurants.

What's Mrs. Grant Looking Forward to?

Mrs. Grant is going to retire this year, and she's really looking forward to her new life. She won't be getting up early every morning and taking the bus to work. She'll be able to sleep late every day of the week. She'll read books, she'll work in her garden, and she'll go to museums with her friends. And she's very happy that she'll be able to spend more time with her grandchildren. She'll take them to the park to feed the birds, she'll take them to the zoo to see the animals, and she'll baby-sit when her son and daughter-in-law go out on Saturday nights.

Page 35 Exercise E

Listen to each question and then complete the answer.

Ex. Does your brother like to swim?

1. Are you going to buy donuts tomorrow?
2. Will Jennifer and John see each other again soon?
3. Doctor, did I sprain my ankle?
4. Does Tommy have a black eye?
5. Is your daughter practicing the violin?
6. Do you and your husband go to the movies very often?

7. Does Diane go out with her boyfriend every Saturday evening?
8. Will you and your wife be visiting us tonight?

Page 36 Exercise B

Listen and choose the word you hear.

1. I've ridden them for many years.
2. Yes. I've taken French.
3. I'm giving injections.
4. I've driven one for many years.
5. Yes. I've written it.
6. I'm drawing it right now.
7. I've spoken it for many years.
8. Yes. I've drawn that.

Page 37 Exercise D

Is Speaker B answering Yes *or* No*? Listen to each conversation and circle the correct answer.*

1. A. Do you know how to drive a bus?
   B. I've driven a bus for many years.
2. A. I usually take the train to work. Do you also take the train?
   B. Actually, I've never taken the train to work.
3. A. Are you a good swimmer?
   B. To tell the truth, I've never swum very well.
4. A. Did you get up early this morning?
   B. I've gotten up early every morning this week.
5. A. I'm going to give my dog a bath today. Do you have any advice?
   B. Sorry. I don't. I've never given my dog a bath.
6. A. Do you like to eat sushi?
   B. Of course! I've eaten sushi for many years.
7. A. I just got a big raise! Did you also get one?
   B. Actually, I've never gotten a raise.
8. A. I did very well on the math exam. How about you?
   B. I've never done well on a math exam.

Page 47 Exercise O

What things have these people done? What haven't they done? Listen and check Yes *or* No.

1. A. Carla, have you done your homework yet?
   B. Yes, I have. I did my homework this morning.
   A. And have you practiced the violin?
   B. No, I haven't practiced yet. I promise I'll practice this afternoon.
2. A. Kevin?
   B. Yes, Mrs. Blackwell?
   A. Have you written your report yet?
   B. No, I haven't. I'll write it immediately.
   A. And have you sent a fax to the Crane Company?
   B. No, I haven't. I promise I'll send them a fax after I write the report.
3. A. Have you fed the dog yet?
   B. Yes, I have. I fed him a few minutes ago.
   A. Good. Well, I guess we can leave for work now.
   B. But we haven't eaten breakfast yet!
4. A. I'm leaving now, Mr. Green.
   B. Have you fixed the pipes in the basement, Charlie?
   A. Yes, I have.
   B. And have you repaired the washing machine?
   A. Yes, I have. It's working again.
   B. That's great! Thank you, Charlie.
   A. I'll send you a bill, Mr. Green.
5. A. You know, we haven't done the laundry all week.
   B. I know. We should do it today.
   A. We also haven't vacuumed the rugs!
   B. We haven't?
   A. No, we haven't.
   B. Oh. I guess we should vacuum them today.
6. A. Are we ready for the party?
   B. I think so. We've gotten all the food at the supermarket, and we've cleaned the house from top to bottom!
   A. Well, I guess we're ready for the party!
7. A. Have you spoken to the landlord about our broken light?
   B. Yes, I have. I spoke to him this morning.
   A. What did he say?
   B. He said we should call an electrician.
   A. Okay. Let's call Ajax Electric.
   B. Don't worry. I've already called them, and they're coming this afternoon.
8. A. Have you hooked up the new VCR yet?
   B. I can't do it. It's really difficult.
   A. Have you read the instructions?
   B. Yes, I have. I've read them ten times, and I still can't understand them!

Page 56 Exercise E

Listen and choose the correct answer.

1. Bob has been engaged since he got out of the army.
2. My sister Carol has been a professional musician since she finished music school.
3. Michael has been home since he fell and hurt himself last week.
4. My wife has gotten up early every morning since she started her new job.
5. Richard has eaten breakfast in the school cafeteria every morning since he started college.
6. Nancy and Tom have known each other for five and a half years.
7. My friend Charlie and I have played soccer every weekend since we were eight years old.

8. Patty has had short hair since she was a teenager.
9. Ron has owned his own business since he moved to Chicago nine years ago.
10. I've been interested in astronomy for the past eleven years.
11. I use my personal computer all the time. I've had it since I was in high school.
12. Alan has had problems with his house since he bought it fifteen years ago.

Page 61 Exercise L

Listen and choose the correct answer.

1. A. Have you always been a salesperson?
   B. No. I've been a salesperson for the past four years. Before that, I was a cashier.
2. A. How long has your daughter been in medical school?
   B. She's been in medical school for the past two years.
3. A. Have your parents always lived in a house?
   B. No. They've lived in a house for the past ten years. Before that, they lived in an apartment.
4. A. How long have you wanted to be an actor?
   B. I've wanted to be an actor since I was in college. Before that, I wanted to be a musician.
5. A. Do you and your husband still exercise at your health club every day?
   B. No. We haven't done that for a year.
6. A. Has James been a bachelor all his life?
   B. No, he hasn't. He was married for ten years.
7. A. Has your sister Jane always wanted to be a writer?
   B. Yes, she has. She's wanted to be a writer all her life.
8. A. Have you ever broken your ankle?
   B. No. I've sprained it a few times, but I've never broken it.
9. A. Have you always liked classical music?
   B. No. I've liked classical music for the past few years. Before that, I liked rock music.
10. A. Has Billy had a sore throat for a long time?
    B. He's had a sore throat for the past two days. Before that, he had a fever.
11. A. Jennifer has been the store manager since last fall.
    B. What did she do before that?
    A. She was a salesperson.
12. A. Have you always been interested in modern art?
    B. No. I've been interested in modern art since I moved to Paris a few years ago. Before that, I was only interested in sports.

Page 64 Exercise E

Listen and choose the correct time expressions to complete the sentences.

1. A. How long have you been living there?
   B. I've been living there since . . .
2. A. How long has your daughter been practicing the piano?
   B. She's been practicing for . . .
3. A. How long have I been running?
   B. You've been running since . . .
4. A. How long have you been feeling bad?
   B. I've been feeling bad for . . .
5. A. How long have they been waiting?
   B. They've been waiting for . . .
6. A. How long has your son been studying?
   B. He's been studying since . . .
7. A. How long have your sister and her boyfriend been dating?
   B. They've been dating since . . .
8. A. Dad, how long have we been driving?
   B. Hmm. I think we've been driving for . . .
9. A. How long has your little girl been crying?
   B. She's been crying for . . .

Page 67 Exercise H

Listen and choose what the people are talking about.

1. She's been directing it for an hour.
2. We've been rearranging it all morning.
3. I've been paying them on time.
4. He's been playing them for years.
5. Have you been bathing them for a long time?
6. They've been rebuilding it for a year.
7. She's been writing it for a week.
8. He's been translating them for many years.
9. I've been reading it all afternoon.
10. She's been knitting them for a few weeks.
11. We've been listening to them all afternoon.
12. I've been recommending it for years.
13. They've been repairing it all day.
14. She's been taking it all morning.
15. I've been solving them all my life.

Page 71 Exercise L

Listen and decide where the conversation is taking place.

1. A. I'm really tired.
   B. No wonder! You've been chopping tomatoes for the past hour.
2. A. Mark! I'm surprised. You've been falling asleep in class all morning, and you've never fallen asleep in class before.
   B. I'm sorry, Mrs. Applebee. It won't happen again.

3. A. I've been washing these shirts for the past half hour, and they still aren't clean.
   B. Here. Try this Presto Soap.

4. A. We've been standing in line for an hour and forty-five minutes.
   B. I know. I hope the movie is good. I've never stood in line for such a long time.

5. A. What seems to be the problem, Mr. Jones?
   B. My back has been hurting me for the past few days.
   A. I'm sorry to hear that.

6. A. You know, we've been reading here for more than two hours.
   B. You're right. I think it's time to go now.

7. A. Do you want to leave?
   B. I think so. We've seen all the paintings here.

8. A. How long have you been exercising?
   B. For an hour and a half.

9. A. We've been waiting for an hour, and it still isn't here.
   B. I know. I'm going to be late for work.

10. A. I think we've seen them all. Which one do you want to buy?
    B. I like that black one over there.

11. A. We've been watching this movie for the past hour, and it's terrible!
    B. You're right. Let's change the channel.

12. A. I've got a terrible headache.
    B. Why?
    A. Customers have been complaining all morning.
    B. What have they been complaining about?
    A. Some people have been complaining about our terrible products, but most people have been complaining about our high prices.

Page 77 Exercise F

Listen and choose the correct answer.

1. A. How long has Janet been an actress?
   B. She's been an actress since she graduated from acting school.

2. A. Have you watched the news yet?
   B. Yes. I saw the president, and I heard his speech.

3. A. Have you always lived in Denver?
   B. No. We've lived in Denver since 1995. Before that, we lived in New York.

4. A. Has Dad made dinner yet?
   B. Not yet. He still has to make it.

5. A. How long has your ceiling been leaking?
   B. It's been leaking for more than a week.
   A. Have you called the superintendent?
   B. Yes, I have. I've called him several times.

6. A. Billy is having trouble with his homework.
   B. Has he asked anyone to help him?
   A. No, he hasn't.

Page 87 Exercise N

Listen and choose the correct answer.

1. Dr. Gomez really enjoys . . .
2. Whenever possible, my wife and I try to avoid . . .
3. Next summer I'm going to learn . . .
4. Every day Rita practices . . .
5. My parents have decided . . .
6. I've considered . . .
7. Are you thinking about . . .
8. I'm going to quit . . .
9. Why do you keep on . . .
10. My doctor says I should stop . . .
11. David can't stand . . .
12. Are you going to continue to . . .
13. James doesn't want to start . . .
14. Next semester Kathy is going to begin . . .
15. You know, you can't keep on . . .

Page 97 Exercise J

Listen and choose the correct answer.

1. Steve lost his voice.
2. Is Beverly one of your relatives?
3. We just canceled our trip to South America.
4. Ricky has been failing all of his tests this year.
5. Francine dislocated her shoulder.
6. What did you and your students discuss in class?
7. My girlfriend and I rode on the roller coaster yesterday.
8. Grandma can't chew this piece of steak very well.
9. Jimmy loves my homemade food.
10. Did you see the motorcycles go by?
11. Do you think Mr. Montero will take a day off soon?
12. Amy wanted to ask her boss for a raise, but she got cold feet.
13. Have you heard that Margaret sprained her wrist?
14. I have to make an important decision.
15. I envy you.
16. I feel terrible. Debbie and Dan broke up last week.
17. My ankle hurts a lot.
18. I was heartbroken when I heard what happened.
19. Michael was furious with his neighbors.
20. We went to a recital last night.
21. Tom, don't forget to shine your shoes!
22. My friend Carla is extremely athletic.
23. My husband and I have been writing invitations all afternoon.
24. Charles rented a beautiful tuxedo for his niece's wedding.

Page 99 Exercise D

Listen and choose the correct answer.

Ex. My grandfather likes to . . .

1. Susan says she's going to stop . . .
2. My wife and I are thinking about . . .
3. David is considering . . .
4. I can't stand to . . .
5. You should definitely keep on . . .

Page 105 Exercise G

Listen and choose the correct answer.

1. A. I looked in the refrigerator, and I can't find the orange juice.
   B. That's because we . . .
2. A. I'm frustrated! My computer isn't working today.
   B. I think you forgot to . . .
3. A. What should I do with the Christmas decorations?
   B. I think it's time to . . .
4. A. Should I take these clothes to the cleaner's?
   B. Yes. You should definitely . . .
5. A. Hmm. What does this word mean?
   B. You should . . .
6. A. I have to return this skateboard to my cousin.
   B. When are you going to . . . ?
7. A. This math problem is very difficult.
   B. Maybe I can . . .
8. A. I'll never remember their new telephone number.
   B. You should . . .
9. A. I just spilled milk on the kitchen floor!
   B. Don't worry. I'll . . .

Page 108 Exercise L

Listen and choose the correct answer.

1. I really look up to my father.
2. My brother picks on me all the time.
3. Did you throw away the last can of paint?
4. I still haven't gotten over the flu.
5. Have you heard from your cousin Sam recently?
6. Why did you turn him down?
7. Did your French teacher call on you today?
8. George picked out a new suit for his wedding.
9. I have to drop my sister off at the airport.
10. Everything in the store is 20 percent off this week.
11. This jacket fits you.
12. Did you try on a lot of shoes?

Page 112 Exercise D

Listen and complete the sentences.

1. I missed the bus this morning.
2. I'm allergic to nuts.
3. I'll be on vacation next week.
4. I've never flown in a helicopter.
5. I can speak Chinese.
6. I like to go sailing.
7. I'm not going to the company picnic this weekend.
8. I saw a very good movie last night.
9. I don't go on many business trips.
10. I've been to London several times.
11. I'm not a vegetarian.
12. I should lose a little weight.
13. I can't stop worrying about my health.
14. I hate to drive downtown.
15. I won't be able to go to Nancy's party this Saturday night.

Page 117 Exercise K

Listen and complete the sentences.

1. I missed the bus today, . . .
2. I'm allergic to cats, . . .
3. I'll be on vacation next week, . . .
4. You've never seen a rainbow, . . .
5. I can speak Italian, . . .
6. I like to go sailing, . . .
7. I've been on television several times, . . .
8. I saw an exciting movie last weekend, . . .
9. I won't be in the office tomorrow, . . .
10. We were late, . . .
11. I'm not a vegetarian, . . .
12. I saw the stop sign, . . .
13. I can't swim very well, . . .
14. They have to work overtime this weekend, . . .
15. I won't be able to go to Sam's party this Friday night, . . .
16. I'm not afraid of flying, . . .
17. I haven't eaten breakfast yet, . . .
18. The other students weren't bored, . . .

Page 121 Exercise C

Listen and complete the sentences.

Ex. Nancy knows how to type, . . .

1. I'm interested in science, . . .
2. I won't be home this evening, . . .
3. I own my own business, . . .
4. I've never hooked up a computer, . . .
5. You just got a raise, . . .

ACTIVITY WORKBOOK ANSWER KEY

UNIT 1

WORKBOOK PAGE 2

A. What's Happening?

1. What's, reading, She's reading
2. Where's, going, He's going
3. What's, watching, She's watching
4. What are, cooking, I'm cooking
5. Where are, moving, We're moving
6. Where are, sitting, They're sitting
7. What's, composing, He's composing
8. What are, baking, I'm baking

WORKBOOK PAGE 3

B. On the Phone

1. are
   I'm watching
   Is
   she is, She's taking
2. Are
   They're
   are they
   is doing
   is playing
   What are you
   I'm cooking
3. Is
   he isn't, He's exercising
   She's, She's fixing

WORKBOOK PAGE 4

C. You Decide: *Why Is Today Different?*

1. clean, I'm cleaning, . . .
2. irons, he's ironing, . . .
3. argue, we're arguing, . . .
4. worry, I'm worrying, . . .
5. watches, she's watching, . . .
6. writes, he's writing, . . .
7. take, I'm taking, . . .
8. combs, he's combing, . . .
9. gets up, she's getting up, . . .
10. smiles, he's smiling, . . .
11. bark, they're barking, . . .
12. wears, she's wearing, . . .

WORKBOOK PAGE 5

D. What Are They Saying?

1. Do you recommend
2. Does, bake
3. Does, get up
4. Do, complain
5. Does, speak
6. Does, live
7. Do you watch
8. Does she play
9. Does he practice
10. Do you plant
11. Does he add
12. Do you wear
13. Does she ride
14. Does he jog
15. Do we need
16. Does he iron
17. Do they have

WORKBOOK PAGE 6

E. Puzzle

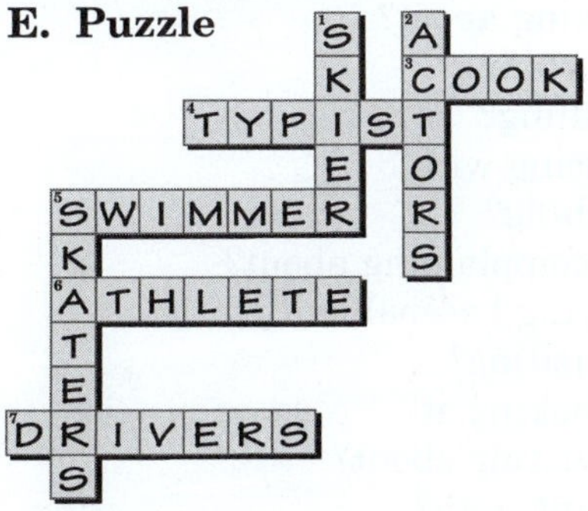

F. What's the Answer?

1. b
2. c
3. b
4. c
5. b
6. c
7. a
8. b

WORKBOOK PAGE 7

G. What Are They Saying?

1. don't, doesn't
   isn't, cook
2. don't, I'm
   drive
3. Do you
   don't, I'm
   You're, type
4. composes, he's
5. isn't, doesn't
   swimmer
6. don't
   speak, speaker

Answers are not provided for the achievement tests. Complete test answer keys are included in *Side by Side Plus* Teacher's Guide 3 and Multilevel Activity & Achievement Test Book 3 (and its accompanying CD-ROM).

H. Listening

1. he does
2. she isn't
3. they are
4. they do
5. she doesn't
6. it is
7. he isn't
8. I do
9. she doesn't
10. he is
11. I'm not
12. we do
13. she is
14. they aren't
15. we don't

WORKBOOK PAGE 9

J. What's the Question?

1. What are you waiting for?
2. Who is he thinking about?
3. What are they ironing?
4. Who are you calling?
5. Who is she dancing with?
6. What's he watching?
7. What are they complaining about?
8. Who is she playing baseball with?
9. Who are they visiting?
10. What are you looking at?
11. What are you writing about?
12. Who is he arguing with?
13. Who is she knitting a sweater for?
14. What are you making?
15. Who are you sending an e-mail to?
16. What are they worrying about?
17. Who is she talking to?
18. Who is he skating with?

WORKBOOK PAGE 10

K. What Are They Saying?

1. your
   We're, them
2. his
   He, them, his
3. they, me
4. her
   She, them
5. your
   I, my
6. your
   I'm, her
7. They, them
8. us, it
9. he, it
10. your
    She, my

WORKBOOK PAGE 11

L. What's the Word?

1. with
2. —
3. at
4. to
5. about
6. —
7. —, with
8. for
9. —

UNIT 2

WORKBOOK PAGE 12

A. Herbert's Terrible Day!

1. had
2. got up
3. ate
4. rushed
5. ran
6. missed
7. waited
8. decided
9. arrived
10. sat
11. began
12. called
13. typed
14. made
15. fixed
16. finished
17. put
18. spilled
19. went
20. ordered
21. felt
22. forgot
23. crashed
24. fell
25. broke
26. hurt
27. left
28. took
29. went

WORKBOOK PAGE 13

B. Listening

1. every day
2. yesterday
3. every day
4. yesterday
5. every day
6. yesterday
7. yesterday
8. every day
9. yesterday
10. every day
11. every day
12. yesterday

C. What's the Word?

1. wanted
2. lifted
3. painted
4. roller-bladed
5. planted
6. needed
7. waited
8. decided

D. Puzzle: *What Did They Do?*

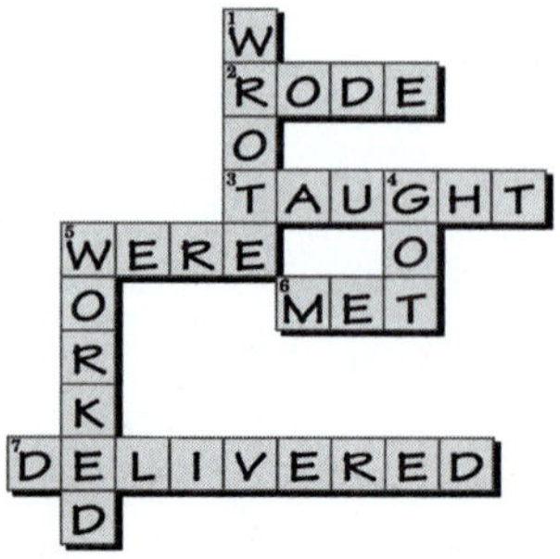

WORKBOOK PAGE 14

E. What's the Question?

1. Did you buy
2. Did they take
3. Did she see
4. Did he speak
5. Did you break
6. Did it begin
7. Did she fly
8. Did you have
9. Did they go
10. Did I sing
11. Did he meet
12. Did you lose

F. What's the Answer?

1. they were bored
2. I wasn't hungry
3. they were tired
4. she wasn't prepared
5. he was angry
6. I wasn't on time
7. she wasn't thirsty
8. I was scared
9. they were sad

WORKBOOK PAGE 15

G. Something Different

1. didn't drive, drove
2. didn't come, came
3. didn't take, took
4. didn't go, went
5. didn't forget, forgot
6. didn't wear, wore
7. didn't teach, taught
8. didn't eat, ate
9. didn't give, gave
10. didn't sit, sat
11. didn't have, had
12. didn't sing, sang

WORKBOOK PAGES 16–17

H. What Are They Saying?

1. Did you
   didn't, was
2. Did you
   didn't
   met
3. Did
   did
   wasn't
4. Did
   she didn't
   weren't
5. Did, fall
   he didn't
   fell
   was
6. Did
   I didn't, rode
   was
   was
7. Did you
   did, was
   didn't
   was
8. Was
   was, Were
   I wasn't, didn't
9. Did
   did
   didn't
   were
10. Did
    they didn't
    danced
    were
11. did
    I did, bought
    Did you
    didn't
    wasn't
12. were
    were
    I was, was
    was
    wasn't

WORKBOOK PAGE 18

I. How Did It Happen?

1. He sprained his ankle while he was playing tennis.
2. She ripped her pants while she was exercising.
3. I broke my arm while I was playing volleyball.
4. He poked himself in the eye while he was fixing his sink.
5. We hurt ourselves while we were skateboarding.
6. They tripped and fell while they were dancing.
7. He burned himself while he was cooking french fries.
8. She got a black eye while she was fighting with the kid across the street.
9. I cut myself while I was chopping carrots.
10. He lost his cell phone while he was jogging in the park.

WORKBOOK PAGE 20

L. What's the Question?

1. Who did you meet?
2. What did she lose?
3. Where did you do your exercises?
4. When did they leave?
5. How did she get here?
6. Where did he sing?
7. How long did they stay?
8. What kind of movie did you see?
9. Why did he cry?
10. Who did she write a letter to?
11. What did they complain about?
12. How many grapes did you eat?
13. Where did he speak?
14. How long did they lift weights?
15. Who did she give a present to?
16. What kind of pie did you order?
17. How many videos did you rent?
18. Who did they send an e-mail to?
19. When did he fall asleep?
20. When did you lose your hat?

WORKBOOK PAGES 21–22

M. Our Vacation

1. we didn't
did you go
We went
2. we didn't
did you get there
We got there by plane.
3. it didn't
did it leave
It left
4. we didn't
weather did you have
We had
5. we didn't
hotel did you stay in
We stayed in a small hotel.
6. we didn't
food did you eat
We ate Japanese food.
7. we didn't
did you take (with you)
We took
8. we didn't
did you get around the city
We got around the city by taxi.
9. we didn't
did you meet
We met
10. we didn't
did you buy
We bought
11. we didn't
did you speak
We spoke English.
12. we did
money did you spend
We spent . . .

WORKBOOK PAGE 23

N. Sound It Out!

1. these
2. did
3. Rita
4. big
5. green
6. mittens
7. knit
8. Did Rita knit these big green mittens?
9. Greek
10. his
11. Richard
12. every
13. speaks
14. with
15. week
16. sister
17. Richard speaks Greek with his sister every week.

UNIT 3

WORKBOOK PAGE 24

A. What Are They Saying?

1. No, I didn't.
rode
I'm going to ride
2. No, he didn't.
wore
He's going to wear
3. No, she didn't.
gave
She's going to give
4. No, they didn't.
drove
They're going to drive
5. No, we didn't.
had
We're going to have
6. No, I didn't.
went
I'm going to go

7. No, he didn't.
   wrote
   He's going to write
8. No, she didn't.
   left
   She's going to leave

WORKBOOK PAGES 25–26

B. Bad Connections!

1. your dentist going to do
2. are you going to go
3. is she going to move to Alaska
4. What are they going to give you?
5. What are you going to do?
6. When are you going to get married?
7. Who are you going to meet?
8. What are you going to name your new puppy?
9. Why are they going to sell your house?
10. Where are you going to go?
11. Who do you have to call?
12. Why are you going to fire me?

C. Listening

1. b	7. b
2. a	8. a
3. a	9. a
4. b	10. b
5. a	11. b
6. b	12. a

WORKBOOK PAGE 27

D. The Pessimist and the Optimist

1. won't have	you will, You'll
2. will hurt	he won't, He won't
3. won't	she will, She'll
4. will be	she won't, She won't
5. won't lose	you will, You'll
6. will forget	they won't, They won't
7. won't fix	he will, He'll
8. won't	they will, They'll like
9. I'll	you won't, You won't

WORKBOOK PAGE 28

E. What Will Be Happening?

1. she will, She'll be doing
2. I will, I'll be filling out
3. he won't, He'll be working out
4. they will, They'll be cleaning
5. he will, He'll be browsing
6. we will, We'll be watching
7. she won't, She'll be attending
8. it won't, It'll be raining

WORKBOOK PAGE 29

G. What Are They Saying?

1. giving, will you be giving
2. will you be doing, be doing
3. talk, talk, studying
4. having/eating, will you be having/eating

WORKBOOK PAGE 31

I. Whose Is It?

1. yours	5. theirs
2. mine	6. ours
3. his	7. hers
4. hers	8. hers

WORKBOOK PAGES 32–33

K. What Does It Mean?

1. b	13. a
2. c	14. b
3. b	15. a
4. b	16. b
5. a	17. a
6. a	18. b
7. c	19. c
8. b	20. a
9. a	21. c
10. c	22. a
11. a	23. b
12. c	24. c

L. Listening: *Looking Forward*

1. a	6. b
2. c	7. b
3. b	8. a
4. b	9. c
5. c	

WORKBOOK PAGES 34–35

CHECK-UP TEST: Units 1–3

A.

1. are
   dance
2. drives
3. you're
   swimmers
4. I'm
   typist
5. aren't, skiers

B.

1. didn't, was
   spoke
2. didn't
   bought
3. Did
   didn't, got
4. didn't, taught
   was
5. Did
   didn't, talked
   wasn't

C.

1. What are you writing about?
2. What are they going to fix?
3. Where did he hike?
4. When will she be ready?
5. How did they arrive?
6. How long will you be staying?
7. How many people is she going to hire?

D.

1. She's adjusting her satellite dish.
2. He chats online.
3. I'm going to visit my mother-in-law.
4. They delivered groceries.
5. He was baking a cake.
6. I'll take the bus.
7. We'll be watching TV.
8. I was chopping carrots.

E.

1. I am
2. they won't
3. you did
4. he does
5. she isn't
6. we do
7. she doesn't
8. we will

UNIT 4

WORKBOOK PAGE 36

A. For Many Years

1. I've ridden
2. I've flown
3. I've given
4. I've spoken
5. I've taken
6. I've done
7. I've drawn
8. I've written
9. I've driven

B. Listening

1. a
2. b
3. a
4. b
5. b
6. a
7. a
8. b

WORKBOOK PAGE 37

C. I've Never

1. I've never flown
2. I've never gotten
3. I've never ridden
4. I've never drawn
5. I've never written
6. I've never taken
7. I've never sung
8. I've never swum
9. I've never been
10. I've never gone
11. I've never given
12. I've never seen

D. Listening

1. Yes
2. No
3. No
4. Yes
5. No
6. Yes
7. No
8. No

WORKBOOK PAGE 38

E. What Are They Saying?

1. Have you ever gotten
   I got
2. Have you ever ridden
   I rode
3. Have you ever worn
   I wore
4. Have you ever gone
   I went
5. Have you ever given
   I gave
6. Have you ever fallen
   I fell

WORKBOOK PAGE 39

G. What Are They Saying?

1. Have, eaten
   they have, They ate
2. Has, driven
   he has, He drove
3. Has, gone
   she has, She went
4. Have, seen
   we have, We saw
5. Have, taken
   they have, They took
6. Have, spoken
   I have, I spoke
7. Have, written
   you have, You wrote
8. Have, met
   we have, We met

WORKBOOK PAGE 40

H. Not Today

1. They've, eaten
   They ate
2. She's, gone
   She went
3. He's, worn
   He wore
4. We've, done
   We did
5. He's, given
   He gave
6. I've, seen
   I saw
7. We've, bought
   We bought
8. She's, visited
   She visited
9. He's, taken
   He took

WORKBOOK PAGE 41

I. What's the Word?

1. go
2. went
3. gone
4. seen
5. saw
6. see
7. ate
8. eaten
9. eat
10. write
11. written
12. wrote
13. wear
14. worn
15. wore
16. spoke

17. speak
18. spoken
19. driven
20. drive
21. drove
22. do
23. did
24. done

WORKBOOK PAGES 42–43

J. What Are They Saying?

1. I've, done
   I did
   have, written
   I have
2. I've, swum
   I swam
3. I've, taken
   I took
   Have, taken
   I have, took
4. He's, gotten
   He got
5. We've, eaten
   We ate
   eaten
6. I've, spoken
   I spoke

WORKBOOK PAGES 44–45

L. In a Long Time

1. I haven't ridden
2. haven't bought
3. I haven't flown
4. I haven't taken
5. I haven't swum
6. hasn't eaten
7. hasn't cleaned
8. He hasn't read
9. I haven't studied
10. haven't seen
11. I haven't given
12. He hasn't made
13. haven't gone
14. I haven't danced

M. Puzzle: *What Have They Already Done?*

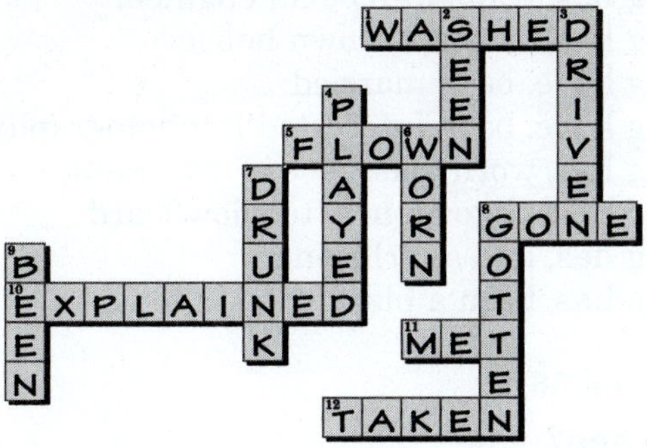

WORKBOOK PAGES 46–47

N. A Lot of Things to Do

1. He's already gone to the supermarket.
2. He hasn't cleaned his apartment yet.
3. He's already gotten a haircut.
4. He hasn't baked a cake yet.
5. He's already fixed his CD player.
6. She's already taken a shower.
7. She hasn't done her exercises yet.
8. She hasn't fed the cat yet.
9. She's already walked the dog.
10. She hasn't eaten breakfast yet.
11. They haven't done their laundry yet.
12. They've already gotten their paychecks.
13. They've already paid their bills.
14. They haven't packed their suitcases yet.
15. They haven't said good-bye to their friends yet.
16. She's already written to Mrs. Lane.
17. She's already called Mr. Sanchez.
18. She hasn't met with Ms. Wong yet.
19. She hasn't read her e-mail yet.
20. She's already sent a fax to the Ace Company.

O. Listening

	Yes	*No*		*Yes*	*No*
1.	✓		5.		✓
		✓			✓
2.		✓	6.	✓	
		✓		✓	
3.	✓		7.	✓	
		✓		✓	
4.	✓		8.		✓
	✓			✓	

WORKBOOK PAGES 48–49

P. What Are They Saying?

1. have, spoke
   did
   flown
2. Have
   haven't, saw
   see
   seen
3. taken
   took
   Have, sent
   sent
   Have, given
4. Have
   have, went
   Have, gone/been
   have, I went/was

5. did
gave
are you going to buy
spent
did you
bought
listen
6. I'm not, taken
got
Have
I have, ate
washed/done

WORKBOOK PAGE 50

R. _J_ulia's Broken Keyboard

1.

> _J_udy,
> Have you seen my blue and _y_ellow _j_acket at _y_our house? I think I left it there _y_esterday after the _j_azz concert. I've looked everywhere, and I _j_ust can't find it anywhere.
> _J_ulia

2.

> Dear _J_ennifer,
> We're sorry _y_ou haven't been able to visit us this _y_ear. Do _y_ou think _y_ou could come in _J_une or _J_uly? We really en_j_oyed _y_our visit last _y_ear. We really want to see _y_ou again.
> _J_ulia

3.

> _J_eff,
> _J_ack and I have gone out _j_ogging, but we'll be back in _j_ust a few minutes. Make _y_ourself comfortable. _Y_ou can wait for us in the _y_ard. We haven't eaten lunch _y_et. We'll have some _y_ogurt and orange _j_uice when we get back.
> _J_ulia

4.

> Dear _J_ane,
> We _j_ust received the beautiful pa_j_amas _y_ou sent to _J_immy. Thank _y_ou very much. _J_immy is too _y_oung to write to _y_ou himself, but he says "Thank _y_ou." He's already worn the pa_j_amas, and he's en_j_oying them a lot.
> _J_ulia

5.

> Dear _J_anet,
> _J_ack and I are coming to visit _y_ou and _J_ohn in New _Y_ork. We've been to New _Y_ork before, but we haven't visited the Statue of Liberty or the Empire State Building _y_et. See _y_ou in _J_anuary or maybe in _J_une.
> _J_ulia

6.

> Dear _J_oe,
> We got a letter from _J_ames last week. He has en_j_oyed college a lot this _y_ear. His favorite sub_j_ects are German and _J_apanese. He's looking for a _j_ob as a _j_ournalist in _J_apan, but he hasn't found one _y_et.
> _J_ulia

WORKBOOK PAGE 51

S. *Is* or *Has*?

1. has
2. is
3. is
4. has
5. is
6. is
7. has
8. is
9. is
10. has
11. is
12. has
13. is
14. has
15. has
16. is
17. has
18. is
19. is
20. has

UNIT 5

WORKBOOK PAGE 52

A. How Long?

1. I've had a headache since
2. They've been married for
3. He's owned a motorcycle since
4. She's been interested in astronomy for
5. I've had a cell phone since
6. We've known each other since
7. They've had a dog for
8. I've had problems with my upstairs neighbor for
9. She's been a computer programmer since
10. He's played in the school orchestra since
11. There have been mice in our attic for

WORKBOOK PAGE 53

B. What's the Question?

1. How long has, wanted to be an engineer
2. How long has, owned his own house
3. How long have, been married
4. How long have, been interested in photography
5. How long has, worn glasses
6. How long have, known how to snowboard
7. How long has, had a girlfriend
8. How long has, been a pizza shop in town

WORKBOOK PAGE 55

D. Since When?

1. I'm
I've been sick

2. has
   She's had
3. knows
   He's known
4. They're
   They've been
5. We're
   We've been
6. have
   I've had
7. It's
   It's been
8. plays
   She's
9. is
   He's been
10. I'm
    I've been

WORKBOOK PAGE 56

E. Listening

1.	b	**7.**	a
2.	b	**8.**	b
3.	a	**9.**	b
4.	b	**10.**	a
5.	a	**11.**	b
6.	a	**12.**	a

F. Crossword

WORKBOOK PAGE 57

G. Scrambled Sentences

1. Julie has liked jazz since she was a teenager.
2. He's known how to play the piano since he was a little boy.
3. I've been interested in astronomy since I was young.
4. They've been engaged since they finished college.
5. He's been a chef since he graduated from cooking school.
6. She's wanted to be a teacher since she was eighteen years old.
7. They've owned their own business since they moved here a year ago.

WORKBOOK PAGE 58

I. Then and Now

1. walk
   They've walked
   they
   walked
2. speaks
   He's spoken
   he spoke
3. is
   She's been
   she was
4. taught
   he teaches
   He's taught
5. has
   visited
   visited
   visit
6. has
   She's had
   had

WORKBOOK PAGE 59

J. Looking Back

1. has Victor been
   He's been a musician, 1990
2. was he
   He was a photographer, 7 years
3. has Mrs. Sanchez taught
   She's taught science, 1995
4. did she teach
   She taught math, 9 years
5. did your grandparents have
   They had a cat, 11 years
6. have they had
   They've had a dog, 1998
7. has Betty worked
   She's worked at the bank, 2000
8. did she work
   She worked at the mall, 2 years
9. did your parents live
   They lived in New York, 20 years
10. have they lived
    They've lived in Miami, 2001

WORKBOOK PAGE 61

L. Listening

1.	b	**7.**	b
2.	b	**8.**	a
3.	a	**9.**	b
4.	b	**10.**	b
5.	b	**11.**	b
6.	a	**12.**	a

UNIT 6

WORKBOOK PAGE 62

A. What's the Word?

1. since
2. for
3. for
4. since
5. since
6. for
7. since
8. for

B. Choose

1. a
2. b
3. b
4. a
5. b
6. b

WORKBOOK PAGE 63

C. How Long?

1. I've been studying since
2. She's been feeling sick for
3. He's been having problems with his car for
4. They've been arguing since
5. We've been waiting for
6. It's been ringing since
7. He's been talking for
8. They've been dating since
9. I've been teaching since
10. You've been chatting online for

WORKBOOK PAGE 64

D. What Are They Doing?

1. is looking
   He's been looking
2. is jogging
   She's been jogging
3. is barking
   It's been barking
4. are planting
   They've been planting
5. is doing
   He's been doing
6. is browsing
   She's been browsing
7. are assembling
   They've been assembling
8. baking
   I've been baking
9. are making
   You've been making

E. Listening

1. a
2. b
3. a
4. b
5. b
6. a
7. b
8. a
9. b

WORKBOOK PAGES 66–67

G. What Are They Saying?

1. Have you been waiting
   have
   I've been waiting
2. Has it been snowing
   it has
   It's been snowing
3. Has he been taking
   he has
   He's been taking
4. Have you been working
   I haven't
   been working
5. Has, been making
   it has
   It's been making
6. Have you been vacuuming
   I have
   I've been vacuuming
7. Have they been studying
   they have
   They've been studying
8. Have we been running
   have
   We've been running
9. Have you been wearing
   I haven't
   I've been wearing
10. Have you been playing
    I haven't
    I've been playing

H. Listening

1. a
2. b
3. b
4. a
5. b
6. b
7. a
8. a
9. b
10. a
11. b
12. a
13. b
14. a
15. b

WORKBOOK PAGE 68

I. Sound It Out!

1. interested
2. is
3. Steve's
4. in
5. history
6. sister
7. very
8. Chinese
9. Steve's sister is very interested in Chinese history.

10. receive
11. this
12. any
13. Peter
14. week
15. didn't
16. e-mail
17. Peter didn't receive any e-mail this week.

WORKBOOK PAGES 70–71

K. What's Happening?

1. We've been eating
   We've, eaten
   We haven't eaten
2. She's been seeing
   She's, see
   She hasn't seen
3. He's been swimming
   He's, swum
4. She's been going
   She's, gone
5. He's been talking
   He's, talked
   he hasn't talked
6. They've been writing
   They've, written
   they haven't written
7. he's been making
   He's, made
   He hasn't made
8. She's been studying
   She's, studied
   she hasn't studied
9. He's been reading
   He's, read
   he hasn't read
10. They've been complaining
    They've, complained
    haven't complained

L. Listening

1. a	7. b
2. b	8. a
3. b	9. b
4. a	10. b
5. a	11. a
6. b	12. b

WORKBOOK PAGE 72

M. Which Word?

1. leaking	7. given
2. flying	8. taken
3. run	9. gone
4. made	10. has been ringing
5. have you been	11. singing
6. see	

WORKBOOK PAGE 74

O. A New Life

1. He's never lived in a big city
2. He's never taken English lessons
3. He's never taken the subway
4. He's never shopped in American supermarkets
5. He's never eaten American food
6. He's never played American football

8. They've been living in a big city
9. They've been taking English lessons
10. They've been taking the subway
11. They've been shopping in American supermarkets
12. They've been eating American food
13. They've been playing American football

WORKBOOK PAGES 76–77

CHECK-UP TEST: Units 4–6

A.

1. have, eaten	4. has, gone
2. hasn't taken	5. haven't paid
3. haven't written	6. has, had

B.

1. Have you spoken	4. Has he, flown
2. Has he ridden	5. Has she, been
3. Have they gotten	6. Have you met

C.

1. It's been sunny	5. They've been arguing
2. We've been browsing	6. I've known
3. She's had	7. She's been
4. He's been studying	8. We've been cleaning

D.

1. She's been working at the bank since
2. They've been barking for
3. It's been snowing for
4. I've wanted to be an astronaut since

E.

1. He's owned
   he owned
2. I've been
   I was
3. She's liked
   she liked

F.

1. b	4. a
2. a	5. a
3. b	6. b

UNIT 7

WORKBOOK PAGE 78

A. What Do They {Enjoy Doing / Like to Do}?

1. enjoy
2. likes to, Talking
3. enjoy
4. like to, Knitting
5. enjoy
6. likes to, delivering
7. enjoy, being
8. likes to, planting
9. enjoys, chatting
10. like to, playing
11. enjoy
12. likes to, going
13. enjoy

WORKBOOK PAGE 80

C. What's the Word?

1. complain
2. sitting
3. eat
4. clean
5. wear
6. cleaning
7. go
8. going
9. sit
10. complaining
11. eating
12. wearing

WORKBOOK PAGE 82

F. My Energetic Grandfather

1. to play/playing
2. to play
3. play

WORKBOOK PAGE 83

H. Choose

1. to buy
2. moving
3. going
4. changing
5. get
6. retiring

WORKBOOK PAGE 85

K. What's the Word?

1. rearranging
2. eating
3. worrying
4. to get/getting
5. to exercise/exercising
6. to ask/asking
7. arguing
8. to take/taking
9. paying, to pay/paying
10. to fall/falling

L. Good Decisions

1. biting
2. to do/doing
3. to cook
4. to cook/cooking
5. paying
6. cleaning
7. gossiping
8. interrupting

WORKBOOK PAGE 86

M. Problems!

1. falling
   falling
2. to lift/lifting
   to lift/lifting
   lifting
3. to tease/teasing
   teasing
   crying
   teasing
4. driving
   to drive/driving
   to drive/driving
5. dressing
   to dress/dressing
   dressing
6. stepping
   to dance/dancing
   going

WORKBOOK PAGE 87

N. Listening

1. a
2. a
3. b
4. b
5. a
6. a
7. b
8. b
9. a
10. b
11. b
12. b
13. a
14. a
15. b

O. What Does It Mean?

1. b
2. c
3. a
4. b
5. c
6. a
7. b
8. a
9. c
10. b
11. b
12. c

UNIT 8

WORKBOOK PAGE 88

A. Before

1. had eaten
2. had, gotten
3. had, visited
4. had driven
5. had, cut
6. had spent
7. had, gone
8. had made
9. had seen
10. had, left
11. had had
12. had, given
13. had lost

WORKBOOK PAGE 90

C. Late for Everything

1. had, left
2. had, begun
3. had, gone---
4. had, closed
5. had, started
6. had, left
7. had, arrived

WORKBOOK PAGE 91

D. In a Long Time

1. hadn't listened
2. hadn't seen
3. hadn't had
4. hadn't gone
5. hadn't remembered
6. hadn't ironed, hadn't shaved
7. hadn't lost
8. hadn't skied
9. hadn't gotten
10. hadn't taken off
11. hadn't studied
12. hadn't ridden

WORKBOOK PAGES 92–93

E. Working Hard

1. She was studying for her science test.
2. She had already written an English composition.
3. She hadn't practiced the trombone yet.
4. She hadn't read the next history chapter yet.
5. She hadn't memorized her lines for the school play yet.
6. He was hooking up the new printer.
7. He had already sent an e-mail to the boss.
8. He had already given the employees their paychecks.
9. He hadn't written to the Bentley Company yet.
10. He hadn't taken two packages to the post office yet.
11. They were cleaning the garage.
12. They had already assembled Billy's new bicycle.
13. They had already fixed the fence.
14. They hadn't repaired the roof yet.
15. They hadn't started to build a tree house yet.
16. She was playing squash.
17. She had already done yoga.
18. She had already gone jogging
19. She hadn't lifted weights yet.
20. She hadn't swum across the pool 10 times yet.

WORKBOOK PAGE 94

F. What Had They Been Doing?

1. had been talking
2. had been living
3. had been working
4. had been going out
5. had been planning
6. had been thinking about
7. had been getting
8. had been borrowing
9. had been eating
10. had been rehearsing
11. had been looking forward
12. had been training
13. had been arriving

WORKBOOK PAGE 96

I. Marylou's Broken Keyboard

1.

Roger,

I'm afraid there's something wrong with the fireplace in the living room. Also, the refrigerator is broken. I've been calling the landlord for three days on his cell phone, but he hasn't called back. I hope he calls me tomorrow.

Marylou

2.

Louise,

I'm terribly worried about my brother Larry's health. He hurt his leg while he was playing baseball. He had already dislocated his shoulder while he was surfing last Friday. According to his doctor, he is also having problems with his blood pressure and with his right wrist. He really should try to relax and take life a little easier.

Marylou

3.

Arnold,

Can you possibly recommend a good restaurant in your neighborhood? I'm planning on taking my relatives to lunch tomorrow, but I'm not sure where.

We ate at a very nice Greek restaurant near your apartment building last month, but I haven't been able to remember the name. Do you know the place?

Your friend,
Marylou

4.

Rosa,

I have been planning a trip to Florida. I'll be flying to Orlando on Friday, and I'll be returning three days later. Have you ever been there? I remember you had family members who lived in Florida several years ago.

Please write back.

All my love,
Marylou

WORKBOOK PAGE 97

J. Listening

1. c
2. b
3. c
4. b
5. c
6. b
7. a
8. b
9. c
10. b
11. a
12. c
13. b
14. a
15. c
16. c
17. b
18. c
19. b
20. a
21. b
22. c
23. a
24. c

WORKBOOK PAGES 98–99

CHECK-UP TEST: Units 7–8

A.

1. eating
2. wrestling
3. to stop
4. boxing
5. Swimming
6. to skate
7. talking
8. doing

B.

1. hadn't spoken
2. had, done
3. had, left
4. hadn't written
5. hadn't had
6. hadn't taken
7. hadn't eaten
8. hadn't gone

C.

1. had been working
2. had been training
3. had been arguing
4. had been planning

D.

1. b
2. a
3. b
4. b
5. a

UNIT 9

WORKBOOK PAGE 100

A. What Are They Saying?

1. pick him up
2. turned it on
3. take them back
4. fill them out
5. hang it up
6. hook it up
7. throw them out
8. took it back
9. took them down
10. call her up

WORKBOOK PAGE 101

B. What Are They Saying?

1. turn on
   turn it on
2. hand, in
   hand it in
3. wake up
   wake them up
4. turn, off
   turn it off
5. take off
   take them off
6. put, away
   put them away
7. Put, on
   put them on
8. bring, back
   bring her back

WORKBOOK PAGE 103

D. What Are They Saying?

1. do it over
2. gave it back
3. hook it up
4. think it over

5. look it up
6. turn him down
7. throw them away
8. written it down
9. cross them out
10. turned it off

WORKBOOK PAGE 104

E. What's the Word?

1. put away
2. hook up
3. take back
4. wake up
5. call up
6. write down
7. clean up
8. put away
9. throw out
10. hang up

WORKBOOK PAGE 105

F. What Should They Do?

1. think it over
2. give it back
3. used it up
4. look it up
5. figure it out
6. wake them up
7. turn it off
8. throw them out

G. Listening

1. b
2. b
3. a
4. b
5. b
6. a
7. b
8. a
9. b

WORKBOOK PAGE 106

H. Come Up With the Right Answer

1. take after
   take after him
2. heard from
   hear from him
3. called on
   call on me
4. looking through
   looked through them
5. got over
   got over it
6. look up to
   look up to me
7. ran into
   ran into her
8. get along with
   get along with her
9. picks on
   picks on them

WORKBOOK PAGE 107

J. Choose

1. b
2. a
3. b
4. b
5. a
6. b
7. b
8. a
9. a
10. b
11. a
12. a
13. b
14. b

WORKBOOK PAGE 108

K. What Does It Mean?

1. b
2. c
3. b
4. c
5. a
6. a
7. b
8. c

L. Listening

1. c
2. b
3. c
4. a
5. b
6. c
7. a
8. c
9. c
10. b
11. a
12. b

UNIT 10

WORKBOOK PAGE 109

A. Not the Only One

1. did I
2. I do
3. can I
4. I am
5. I will
6. was I
7. am I
8. I have
9. I did
10. will I
11. do I

WORKBOOK PAGE 110

B. What a Coincidence!

1. do I
2. I do
3. I did
4. have I
5. I will
6. did I
7. I was
8. I did
9. I am
10. do I
11. am I

WORKBOOK PAGE 111

C. Not the Only One

1. did I
2. I'm not
3. was I
4. I can't
5. I won't
6. have I
7. I can't
8. am I
9. I didn't
10. do I
11. will I

WORKBOOK PAGE 112

D. Listening

1. did I
2. I am
3. will I
4. I haven't
5. I can
6. I do
7. am I
8. I did
9. do I
10. have I
11. I'm not
12. I should
13. can I
14. do I
15. I won't

WORKBOOK PAGE 113

G. What Are They Saying?

1. did he
2. will she
3. he was
4. has she
5. you should
6. they were
7. so can
8. did he
9. I do
10. . . ., so has

WORKBOOK PAGE 114

H. What Are They Saying?

1. can I
2. they didn't
3. is he
4. she doesn't
5. were they
6. she hasn't
7. will they
8. aren't either
9. neither has
10. she hadn't

WORKBOOK PAGE 115

I. What Are They Saying?

1. so did she
   she did, too
2. neither could he
   he couldn't either
3. so does he
   he does, too
4. neither does she
   she doesn't either
5. neither had she
   she hadn't either
6. so is he
   he is, too

WORKBOOK PAGE 116

J. Our Family

1. aren't, been
2. is, playing, doing
3. can, drawing, was
4. doesn't, going
5. isn't, has been taking
6. haven't, lived, for, lived
7. doesn't, hasn't spoken
8. won't, hasn't
9. does, sung, since
10. aren't, up, away
11. doesn't, for
12. aren't, skating, had, skated

WORKBOOK PAGE 117

K. Listening

1. didn't
2. isn't
3. won't
4. have
5. can't
6. doesn't
7. haven't
8. didn't
9. will
10. wasn't
11. is
12. didn't
13. can
14. don't
15. will
16. is
17. have
18. was

WORKBOOK PAGE 118

M. Sound It Out!

1. cooks
2. too
3. shouldn't
4. put
5. cookies
6. good
7. sugar
8. Good cooks shouldn't put too much sugar in their cookies.
9. two
10. books
11. bookcase
12. who
13. took
14. afternoon
15. Susan's
16. Who took two books from Susan's bookcase this afternoon?

WORKBOOK PAGE 119

N. What Does It Mean?

1.	j	**14.**	a
2.	c	**15.**	u
3.	q	**16.**	l
4.	s	**17.**	p
5.	n	**18.**	e
6.	h	**19.**	o
7.	i	**20.**	k
8.	x	**21.**	f
9.	m	**22.**	t
10.	v	**23.**	z
11.	w	**24.**	g
12.	y	**25.**	d
13.	b	**26.**	r

WORKBOOK PAGES 120–121

CHECK-UP TEST: Units 9–10

A.

1. it in
2. up to him
3. from her
4. it over
5. it up
6. out of it
7. for it
8. them up
9. them out
10. it down
11. over it

B.

1. so is
2. neither will
3. were, too
4. can't either
5. so have
6. did, too
7. neither has
8. so do
9. neither is

C.

1. isn't
2. will
3. doesn't
4. has
5. didn't

Correlation Key

Student Text Pages	Activity Workbook Pages
Chapter 1	
2	2–3
3	4–5
4	6–8
7–8	9–11
	T1–T4 (Test)
Chapter 2	
12	12–13
13	14–17
14–15	18–19
18–19	20–23
	T5–T10 (Test)
Chapter 3	
22–23	24–26
25	27
26	28–29
27	30
28–29	31–33
	T11–T14 (Test)
Check-Up Test	**34–35**
Chapter 4	
38	36
39	37
40	38
41	39
42–43	40–43
45	44–45
46	46–47
48	48–50
50	51
	T15–T18 (Test)
Chapter 5	
52–53	52–54
56–57	55–57
58–59	58–59
62–63	60–61
	T19–T24 (Test)
Chapter 6	
70–71	62–65
72	66–68
74–75	69–71
76–77	72–75
	T25–T30 (Test)
Check-Up Test	**76–77**

Student Text Pages	Activity Workbook Pages
Chapter 7	
82	78–79
84	80–81
86–87	82
88–89	83–84
90–91	85–87
	T31–T36 (Test)
Chapter 8	
96–97	88–89
100	90
101	91
104–105	92–93
106–107	94–96
109	97
	T37–T42 (Test)
Check-Up Test	**98–99**
Chapter 9	
116	100
117	101–102
119	103
122–123	104–105
124	106–107
126–127	108
	T43–T48 (Test)
Chapter 10	
132	109–110
133	111–112
134–135	113
138–139	114–115
141	116–117
143	118–119
	T49–T54 (Test)
Check-Up Test	**120–121**

SIDE by SIDE Activity Workbook Audio Program

The *Side by Side* Activity Workbook Audio CDs contain all workbook listening activities and GrammarRaps for entertaining language practice through rhythm, stress, and intonation. Students can use the Audio Program to extend their language learning through self-study outside the classroom.

Audio Program Contents

Track	Page	Activity
CD 1		
1		Introduction
Chapter 1		
2	p. 7	Exercise H Listening
3	p. 8	Exercise I GrammarRap
Chapter 2		
4	p. 13	Exercise B Listening
5	p. 19	Exercise J GrammarRap
6	p. 19	Exercise K GrammarRap
7	p. 23	Exercise N Sound It Out!
Chapter 3		
8	p. 26	Exercise C Listening
9	p. 30	Exercise H GrammarRap
10	p. 31	Exercise J GrammarRap
11	p. 33	Exercise L Listening
Check-Up Test: Chapters 1–3		
12	p. 35	Exercise E Listening
Chapter 4		
13	p. 36	Exercise B Listening
14	p. 37	Exercise D Listening
15	p. 38	Exercise F GrammarRap
16	p. 43	Exercise K GrammarRap
17	p. 47	Exercise O Listening
18	p. 49	Exercise Q Listening
Chapter 5		
19	p. 54	Exercise C GrammarRap
20	p. 56	Exercise E Listening
21	p. 61	Exercise L Listening
CD 2		
1		Introduction
Chapter 6		
2	p. 64	Exercise E Listening
3	p. 65	Exercise F GrammarRap
4	p. 67	Exercise H Listening
5	p. 68	Exercise I Sound It Out!
6	p. 71	Exercise L Listening
Check-Up Test: Chapters 4–6		
7	p. 77	Exercise F Listening
Chapter 7		
8	p. 79	Exercise B GrammarRap
9	p. 80	Exercise D GrammarRap
10	p. 83	Exercise I GrammarRap
11	p. 87	Exercise N Listening
Chapter 8		
12	p. 89	Exercise B GrammarRap
13	p. 95	Exercise G GrammarRap
14	p. 95	Exercise H Listening
15	p. 97	Exercise J Listening
Check-Up Test: Chapters 7–8		
16	p. 99	Exercise D Listening
Chapter 9		
17	p. 102	Exercise C GrammarRap
18	p. 105	Exercise G Listening
19	p. 107	Exercise I GrammarRap
20	p. 108	Exercise L Listening
Chapter 10		
21	p. 112	Exercise D Listening
22	p. 112	Exercise E GrammarRap
23	p. 112	Exercise F GrammarRap
24	p. 117	Exercise K Listening
25	p. 117	Exercise L GrammarRap
26	p. 118	Exercise M Sound It Out!
Check-Up Test: Chapters 9–10		
27	p. 121	Exercise C Listening